8. 50

As we understood...

A Collection of Spiritual Insights
by
Al-Anon and Alateen Members

Al-Anon Family Group Headquarters, Inc.

For information and catalog of literature write to the
World Service Office for Al-Anon and Alateen:
AL-ANON FAMILY GROUP HEADQUARTERS, INC.
1600 Corporate Landing Parkway
Virginia Beach, VA 23454-5617
Phone: (757) 563-1600 Fax: (757) 563-1655

This book is also available in: Finnish, French, Italian and
Portuguese.

AL-ANON FAMILY GROUP HEADQUARTERS, INC. 1985
*All rights reserved. No part of this publication may be reproduced,
stored in or introduced into a retrieval system or transmitted, in any
form or by any means (electronic, mechanical, photocopying, recording
or otherwise) Without the prior written permission of the publisher.*

Library of Congress Catalog Card No. 85-071379
ISBN-0-910034-56-7

Publisher's Cataloging in Publication

As we understood—: a collection of spiritual insights/by
Al-Anon and Alateen members.

p. cm.
Includes index.
LCCN 85-071379.
ISBN 0-310034-56-7

1. Alcoholics—Rehabilitation. 2. Alcoholics—Family relationships.
3. Children of alcoholics—miscellanea. 4. Al-Anon Family Group
Headquarters. Inc. 5. Alcoholics Anonymous. I. Al-Anon Family
Group Headquarters, inc.

HV5278.A85 1990   362.2'9'3
                                               QB192-20140

 Approved by
World Service Conference
Al-Anon Family Groups

The Al-Anon Family Groups are a fellowship of relatives and friends of alcoholics who share their experience, strength and hope in order to solve their common problems. We believe alcoholism is a family illness and that changed attitudes can aid recovery.

Al-Anon is not allied with any sect, denomination, political entity, organization or institution; does not engage in any controversy, neither endorses nor opposes any cause. There are no dues for membership. Al-Anon is self-supporting through its own voluntary contributions.

Al-Anon has but one purpose: to help families of alcoholics. We do this by practicing the Twelve Steps, by welcoming and giving comfort to families of alcoholics, and by giving understanding and encouragement to the alcoholic.

The Suggested Preamble for the Twelve Steps

The Serenity Prayer

God grant me the serenity
To accept the things I cannot change,
Courage to change the things I can,
And wisdom to know the difference.

Preface

What gives hope to Al-Anon/Alateen members? Many have experienced situations that others would find unbearable, yet they develop strength and hope for the future. "I looked around me at group meetings and saw a few people as hurt and bitter and angry as I was," said one member, "but most were facing life as it came. They were able to accept what I thought were outrageous situations. And I wanted to learn how they did it."

"When I was told that alcoholism was a disease and I was powerless over it, I felt a surge of relief. I was relieved to know there was hope for me," said another. "Gradually, I began to understand that I was witnessing a spiritual growth that I read about in the literature. And one day, I realized that I was looking at the world with new eyes. Instead of seeking only misery and despair, I could see sunshine and happiness. I was making reasoned, conscious choices. Instead of reacting to every feeling, I stopped and examined my contribution to a particular situation. I tried to put myself in another person's position. I said the Serenity Prayer more often and learned to accept the fact that I did not have control over many situations in my life. But I was responsible for changing what I could."

This is how some members describe spiritual growth. Each Al-Anon and Alateen member has a different definition based on different experience. For many, spiritual growth has changed life dramatically. Another member shared, "Al-Anon has given me everything—the desire to live again, love for my fellow man, courage to face any difficult situation, the serenity it takes to accept certain realities and hope for the future."

This collection of sharings on spiritual growth gives us a unique opportunity to learn from the insights of others who have traveled similar paths. Each person's story demonstrates the growth he or she has found in the program. By reading about the spiritual experiences of others, we are given a distant image of what is concrete and life-transforming to those who make the Twelve Steps a part of their everyday lives.

It is only through applying what we learn that we can continue to grow spiritually and change our own lives.

=====Contents=====

1

Fellowship

"When I came to Al-Anon, I had life without living."

Most of us can identify with this statement by an Al-Anon member from Spain. Many of us remember the sense of hopelessness and desperation that we felt when we were newcomers. Our lives had been deeply affected by someone else's drinking and we felt trapped and hurt.

A member from Wisconsin shared her feelings about the isolation and loneliness that often result from being involved with a person who drinks excessively: "For years, I thought the

1

alcoholic in my life was the only person in the world who stomped around the front yard, screaming unfounded accusations and threatening violence to anyone who tried to calm him. After only a few Al-Anon meetings, I learned that others lived with the same frustrating situations, but they had somehow learned not to be frustrated. Whatever they had—whatever presence allowed them to laugh and enjoy life—I wanted. I also wanted their understanding and friendship. I was starving for friends who cared about how I felt. People in Al-Anon didn't offer me solutions, but they listened and I could be honest with them. I didn't have to cover up, make excuses, or pretend that I didn't hurt. They assured me that it was okay to be human and they accepted me just as I was. Slowly, it dawned on me that these people were living a spiritual life, and that is what helped them cope with the problem at hand instead of wallowing in self-pity as I had been doing. With their help, I began to believe that I could spend my energy laughing instead of crying, thanking my Higher Power instead of cursing alcoholism, and developing a plan of action instead of being overwhelmed and paralyzed."

The fellowship of Al-Anon helped us break through the walls of isolation that most of us had built up. We soon learned that others who had been in the same types of situations were able to change their spiritual lives and recover from the isolation and disillusionment that dominated their lives before Al-Anon.

By attending meetings with people who were recovering spiritually, we learned to stop comparing our situations with theirs and began to identify with their feelings. We learned that self-pity was self-defeating and it could paralyze us if we continued to focus on old wounds.

The fellowship offered us tools to live life in the present. We learned that the choices we make today will affect our lives tomorrow. For people whose lives have not been affected by the drinking of others, some of these truths may appear self-evident; but for us, any suggestion for a recovering person was a ray of hope. Most of us wanted to change our lives and get rid of the anxiety and fear that had been our constant companions. People in the fellowship assured us that we could change, that our lives could be healed and that they would gladly share their experiences with us if we would keep coming back.

At the first Al-Anon meeting I attended, a woman told me to take care of myself and let my Higher Power take care of the alcoholic. She assured me that I was not responsible for the drinking and I would not be responsible for sobriety. I could no longer judge the alcoholic because his disease caused him to behave in ways he could not control. What I could do was change myself. It was the first time in my life that someone had given me permission to put myself and my needs first.

After many years of covering up his illness and making excuses for his behavior, I was relieved to be in the company of people who accepted me as I was, and I realized that I could not control the alcoholic's actions. They saw qualities in me that I had ignored for years and helped me give myself credit for my positive attributes.

They welcomed me into the group. I was inspired by the strength that some people showed in times of crisis, and I was awed by the caring and love that people shared with me. After so many years of feeling helpless and worthless, I was in a group that not only accepted me as I was, but helped me become the person I had always wanted to be. They taught me that I could not love and help others until I felt loved and secure myself. Today, with the help of my Higher Power and the fellowship of Al-Anon, I am often able to share that love and support with others who need it.

—*Wisconsin, United States*

When I first arrived in Al-Anon, I was completely without faith, love and belief, not only in regard to other people, but above all, in regard to myself. I was alone with my problem and had completely lost the spirit to live.

After only a few minutes in my first meeting, I realized I was no longer alone. The lost battles that I had fought against the alcoholic in my life were common ground to most of the participants in that meeting, who, like myself, had desperately tried to dominate and control something that is beyond control. I immediately realized that I could not control the alcoholic, but I could take possession and control of my own life with the help of my Higher Power and the fellowship of Al-Anon.

—*Italy*

When I came into Al-Anon in my early thirties, I was spiritually, emotionally, and physically distressed. Coming to meetings on a regular basis gave me almost immediate relief from my more devastating symptoms: paralyzing fear, uncontrollable rages, and a self-loathing that made me wish I were anyone but myself. I learned a great deal about alcoholism and decided to stop drinking myself, just for "health reasons." I had started jogging and stopped smoking, so the decision to stop drinking just seemed like another step in my physical fitness plan. I became self-righteous and angry about the drinkers around me; I could really point the finger at the many alcoholics in my life. Yet, in Al-Anon, I always felt just ever-so-slightly out of place, an outsider. I wondered what the feeling was. I didn't feel the need to make a total commitment to Al-Anon; after all, didn't they say, "take what you need and leave the rest"? So I took the meetings, the slogans, the stories and the sharing because they made my life calmer and easier. And I left the rest: the Steps, a sponsor (I didn't really need one), my own honest sharing. For many years, I was not ready to be honest with myself. What I had forgotten (what I denied), was that before I gave up alcohol for health reasons, I had a fifteen year history of alcoholic drinking myself.

When hanging on the fringes of Al-Anon began to cause enough pain, I immersed myself in the Steps, especially the Third. I prayed for relief. Physically, I had recovered; my health program had been successful and I was feeling fit, but spiritually and emotionally, I was still in trouble. This led me to the Steps, a sponsor and self-honesty. When I finally took the Fourth Step after six years in Al-Anon, I was able to admit my own alcoholism. Through the Fifth Step, I was led to AA and it is with immense gratitude that I say it was the beautiful gift of Al-Anon and its members that began my journey of recovery and hope.

—*Anonymous*

I called my mother one day looking for financial aid and moral support. My one-and-only's alcoholism had finally pushed me to ask my mother to let me come home. She said that I was always welcome at home, but she couldn't help me. She said she had never lived with alcoholism and could give me no real comfort or understanding. But she had seen a television program about the families of alcoholics. From the program, she had learned that alcoholism was a family disease. She asked if we had Al-Anon meetings in my town. I told her I didn't know, but I'd never have the courage to go. I'll never forget her advice: "Before you give up, why don't you go hear what those people have to say?" And I did. I would have done anything she suggested.

I was so desperate I couldn't even use my oldest excuse: "But I'm different." I went to Al-Anon. They listened to me and I listened to them. So much of what was said applied to my life, but that "Higher Power" talk . . . well . . ., they said to take what I needed and leave the rest. I did, but that "Higher Power" seemed to turn up no matter which way I turned. I finally broke down and told my group how I felt. They said to try to think of something stronger, more powerful than myself. I felt so powerless, it should have left me with a multitude of possibilities.

Gradually, I realized that my group gave me hope, laughter, comfort, understanding, freedom and trust. I realized that I did believe in goodness and love and life. I had faith that they could do what I could not. They could help me learn to live again. Whatever powered them was my Higher Power. And their many hands and hearts have helped me become sane.

—*Wyoming, United States*

I had decided a long time back to find a means of preventing my husband from drinking, one way or another, and that's what I was doing. I was holding my husband by one hand and alcoholism had him by the other, so we were going in opposite directions. I had no peace of mind at all because I felt guilt for failing to help the person I loved the most. My first Al-Anon meeting was an unforgettable one, for I learned that alcoholism was a disease. To admit that I was helpless over alcohol was easy enough, but the word "disease" was difficult at first. I thought of viruses, germs and diabetes. I was looking at my husband as a kind of microbe. I couldn't really believe alcoholism was a disease. But by going to meetings every week, by saying the Serenity Prayer often, and with the help of my Higher Power, I came to believe from the bottom of my heart that it is a disease and that we could both recover.

—*Quebec, Canada*

Looking back, I realize that I had my first spiritual experience at my first Al-Anon meeting. Although I know that I walked through those doors on my feet, in my mind's eye, I was crawling on my knees. Tears were running down my cheeks.

The members were not shocked to hear the sordid details of my husband's violence, the visits from the police nor the separations. They reassured me and, as my tears dried, there were smiles on their faces. I left the meeting that night

11

with several phone numbers and a glimmer of the first peace I had known in ages.

I didn't know what it was, but something new had entered my life. I had arrived that night with dead spirits and left with my spirits awakened.
—*New Jersey, United States*

I feel that I am really only twenty-one-and-a-half years old. It has been that long since I walked into my first Al-Anon meeting. I was wrapped up in fear and anxiety, sure I was going insane. I had already had the experience of a mental hospital and was searching for some way to keep sane.

There were ten women in that first meeting. By the time I left, I felt as if a boulder had been lifted from my shoulders. I knew there was a God of love, not punishment. It sounds like a lot to learn in one meeting, but I was ready.

The road has not been a smooth one. There have been many valleys. My husband was killed ten months after my first meeting, but those last ten months were the best we ever had. He continued to drink daily, but thanks to Al-Anon, my attitude changed many things in our home life.

Then I thought, I don't need Al-Anon; I don't have a drinking spouse. It took only a few weeks of staying away from the meetings and a few kind words from an Al-Anon friend to make me realize this fellowship was still of value to me.

Two years later, I married another alcoholic who had been in AA for seven years. It has been shown to me time after time that living with an alcoholic is not the only cause for problems in living.

So many wonderful things have happened that it would take many pages to tell them all. I have been able to Let Go and Let God take care of my adult children. That doesn't mean I agree with everything they do, but I have been able to use the slogan, "Live and Let Live," in this situation. I have been able to release my husband to be his own person. He says he has more freedom than he's ever had, yet we are very close and share many things. I also have been able to find myself and do things I never dreamed I could do.

It all comes down to this: Al-Anon is for me. I make my life what it is. I can have a good day or a bad day. It depends on my attitude. With these Twelve Steps, I can only make progress.

I thank my Higher Power and my alcoholic mother who bought me my first Al-Anon book. I am grateful for these many years of learning and sharing with others.

—*Arizona, United States*

My life was void of such things as mental and emotional sobriety, peace of mind, serenity and unselfish love. Such things cannot enter a life that is cluttered with resentments, self-pity, selfishness, intolerance and all the other defects of character known to those of us who become ill as we do. Then I walked into this flowing mass of love and felt its healing power. Through God's grace, the Al-Anon program and my own efforts, I became whole again. I became part of this love because I was enabled, once more, to love and accept love. Is there a greater blessing?

—*Louisiana, United States*

I was one of those who only came to Al-Anon because I couldn't think of any other place to go. I deeply distrusted every word I heard; after all, no one gives away something for nothing—only fools would believe that. I expected that, any meeting now, someone would tell me about a special workshop that would only cost a hundred dollars to attend, or would ask me to bring a friend.

After many meetings, those initial suspicions gave way and I began to feel some of the caring from seasoned members. This gave rise to a new fear—that I was going to turn into some kind of mass-produced Al-Anon personality. The smiling, serene faces of long-time members seemed somehow, one big blur of moronic happiness. Since much of my life had already been spent rebelling against parents and other authorities, I certainly didn't plan to let Al-Anon turn me into a grinning idiot who could only babble about Steps and serenity.

Eventually, some of my emotions started coming up for inspection, but they weren't pleasant feelings. Fear, anger and resentments that had long lain buried bubbled up uncontrollably, gushing out in endless painful tears at meeting after meeting. It all had to come out.

This catharsis took about two months of daily meetings. For the first time in my life, I found a bit of gratitude and I was thankful because I really felt better.

—*Arizona, United States*

My Higher Power has given me many assets, and I know that they are all gifts. We all have them, though they're different. A friendly smile, a sunny disposition, a quick wit, an eager hand, a sharing nature, a loving heart—all are very special gifts. Although gifts are free, they carry a responsibility to develop them and stretch them to limits we didn't know were possible, all with the help of a Higher Power. Our gifts are neither meant to be held close nor boasted about; they diminish with self-centeredness. They are meant to flourish by free giving. We don't need to envy the gifts of others. Though our own may seem less exciting than another's, they are no less important. Everyone has a place, a job, a uniqueness. We can all use our gifts in the fellowship of Al-Anon.

—New York, United States

As I let go of destructive, negative, critical thinking and behaving and let God come in with His gifts of love, peace, acceptance, tolerance, humility, patience, and understanding, I am learning to walk the path of love shown me by the good people of Al-Anon. In practicing the principles of the program in all my affairs and using God's guidance in making decisions that are right for me, regardless of whether others are pleased or not, I feel myself no longer tied to wanting control and approval. This does not mean that I am inconsiderate of others. What I have found is that when God leads me to make a decision that is right for me, it is also the best thing for everyone around me. And what a neat feeling it is to know that, with God's help, I do have choices, that I can be free, One Day at a Time.

—*Anonymous*

Early in my Al-Anon days, I was aware of a powerful spirit pervading the meetings I attended. It was a spirit of love, goodwill, willingness, understanding and any two or more members could help. I would watch for it to be produced in the meetings. I could see it gradually healing those badly damaged relatives, friends and partners, including myself, and restoring a willingness to try the searching methods suggested, to help their families and themselves. I watched them help the alcoholic through their new understanding, in spite of the often ghastly things that they were subjected to.

—*Australia*

Each and every one of you helped me in countless ways—from a simple thing like a handshake, a hug, or a smile that genuinely said, "I'm glad to see you," to patiently listening to me when I whined and cried, or when you told me what I needed to hear, when it was necessary.

You cared and you shared, oh so willingly, the simple secrets of this program. You showed me how to surrender, then grow slowly from a firm foundation of humility and honesty, One Day at a Time. You showed me that my Higher Power is my partner in my walk through life, if I share with Him all my hopes, fears, joys and sorrows.

You taught me how to pray with honesty and what to pray for: His will for us and the power to carry that out. You showed me time and time again that prayers are answered and miracles do happen everyday. You told me that I always get what I need when I need it—not necessarily things I think I want when I want them. You taught me how to handle resentments and self-pity, the two emotions that were destroying me. You told me, "Gratitude changes your attitude." You taught me how to achieve inner peace and serenity by a faithful, trusting acceptance of my Higher Power's will, especially in the midst of trouble. You never let me forget that this is a life-or-death situation, but paradoxically, you showed me how to laugh and have fun.

In time, you taught me how to reach beyond myself and to think of others and showed me how to treat them. You taught me by example, for you did not take my inventory when I came. Neither did you criticize me when I stumbled; instead, you patiently let me grow at my own pace and encouraged even my most feeble efforts. Then, you taught me how to maintain this wealth of inner perspective—that I must, on a daily basis, take inventory of myself, share it with God as well as others and ask for His guidance. And finally; you taught me how to keep this

unbelievably beautiful way of life full to over-
flowing with inner peace and serenity. "To keep
it, you have to give it away." You gave it to me,
every one of you, each in your own way. I am
eternally grateful because you gave me back my
life and added a quality to it that I did not imagine existed.
—*Indiana, United States*

Today, my Higher Power is my best friend.
When I walk toward Him, and when in my
humanness, I walk away, He is always there with
arms outstretched for a hug, a kiss, a pat on the
back or even a handshake.
—*Kentucky, United States*

I believed in God, yet in my confused state of
mind, I was not able to feel the active presence of
my Higher Power. I knew something was helping; something or someone was comforting, caring for and loving me. Yet, I could not see that it
was my Higher Power. It was only after a com-

ment made at a meeting that I was able to get a clear view of the spiritual nature of the program. One member suggested to another newcomer that she view her Higher Power as "the group." With this insight, I was able to see my Higher Power active in my daily life, and my life took on a stronger, more serene, spiritual nature.

I came to realize that my Higher Power works through the people around me, including Al-Anon members. When I started my day with the Third Step and committed my will and my life to the care of God, I committed myself to listening to others. God was working through them to guide me as He willed. This idea helped me to really open myself up to new people and situations. The disease of alcoholism had caused me to close myself off from the world. Listening and looking for God in others rid me of much of that isolation.

It was the spiritual nature of the program that allowed me to cry out for help, usually to the one group member who could best help me. In the same way, it seemed that a meeting topic often was exactly the one I needed to hear on that day. I've placed a lot of trust in Al-Anon, something I never thought I could do. However, my God has given me this program and its people to help me see and work toward His will for me, and I can trust in that.

Trust, courage, humility, love, confidence and hope are the gifts of the spiritual nature of Al-Anon for me. As long as I remember that things are done in God's time and in God's way, and if I stay open to God working through me and others, days are easier, problems more solvable, and my life is more serene.

—*Wisconsin, United States*

During a period of prayer and meditation, the word "candlepower" came to my mind. We don't take much stock in candles these days because so much of what we use is powered by electricity. But what happens when a power failure plunges us into darkness? The first thing we do is grope for the nearest candle. Any old candle will do. We don't care if it's big or small, what color it is, or where it came from. We light it to dispel the darkness, to keep from banging into the furniture or falling down the stairs. By the light of that one small candle, we're able to round up all the candles we have and if we group them together, the room becomes as bright as day.

I like to think we can be candles. It doesn't matter if we're big or small, what color we are, or where we come from. It doesn't matter if our light is small. When we don't share it with others, we diminish ourselves, spiritually. Each time we feel we're not good enough or wise enough or we just don't care enough to try to help someone else, we put distance between ourselves and our Higher Power.

I'm beginning to understand how the AA and Al-Anon groups are able to work so many miracles in so many lives. By combining our light, we illuminate areas of knowledge and understanding for each other. What's lacking in me can be found in another member of the group. It's this exchange—this giving and receiving of love, faith, hope and joy—that raises our consciousness to a higher level, bringing regeneration and peace into our lives.

—*British Columbia, Canada*

Understanding the language of Al-Anon is a vital part of working the program. Two years ago, the language of my life was loneliness, despair, fear and hopelessness. Today those words are not in my vocabulary, yet I pray never to forget the empty years as each unhappy newcomer attends his or her first meeting. Most are there because of the most wonderful relationship in Al-Anon: sponsorship. I found Al-Anon because a member, still living with an active alcoholic, cared enough to give her phone number to several local agencies.

That Al-Anon can change us from withdrawn, inward-looking individuals into people who joyfully practice "Love thy neighbor" is a miracle we witness often. Today, I believe that Al-Anon sponsorship has no beginning and no end; it is universal love in action. And, most of all, it is a loving God working through the group conscience saying, "I am responsible."

I am responsible whenever a relative or friend of an alcoholic reaches out. I want my hand always to be there. The continued progress of Al-Anon depends on the hands that reach out for help and the hands that give joyfully.

—*New Zealand*

To know that you are human and so am I, to love others enough to give them the rights I would like to have for myself, to hold the hand of one in pain, to have someone say, "I understand"— these are the things spiritual.

—*Arizona, United States*

When a member is new, nothing is expected except his or her own healing; but as time passes, the whirling emotions settle and it is vital to do service for the progress of Al-Anon. Doing service can contribute to our personal growth and development. In this way, we can express our gratitude and repay some of the huge debt we owe to Al-Anon.

—*Texas, United States*

I think that the fellowship of Al-Anon gives us two important qualities that are lacking in many of our lives as a result of living with alcoholics: intimacy and interdependence. We become very close to other members because they understand our predicaments. After we share our inventory with a sponsor, intimacy becomes an important element in the relationship. Most of us had never before experienced the closeness that we have in Al-Anon.

Another aspect of fellowship is that we become interdependent in a very healthy way; we learn that we can contribute to the well-being of others and it can have wonderfully positive results. After so many years of trying to make a positive contribution to the alcoholics in our lives, it is rewarding to share with people who are doing their best to improve their lives. And when we are feeling down or lonely, the caring and sharing of other members is the best remedy in the world.

—*Ohio, United States*

How beautiful is the joy of contributing even a little to the happiness of others.

—*Mexico*

2

Moving Toward A Spiritual Awakening

We have often heard people tell newcomers that Al-Anon is a spiritual, not a religious program. While the principles of our program are spiritual in nature and may overlap some of the purposes of religion, they are not limited to belief in a particular doctrine. In addition to offering healing for a hurt spirit, the fellowship offers empathy and choice. For many, choosing to come to Al-Anon was the beginning of a conscious spiritual journey; the first opportunity to recognize and acknowledge our pain and use the tools others have used to live again.

We learned simple slogans like "First Things First," and began to live "One Day at a Time." Nothing could be gained by reliving old grievances, or by dwelling on what might happen tomorrow. But we could gain enormous peace of mind by realizing that today is the only day we are given. And the fellowship showed us gratitude for life itself. They told us they had followed a plan, the Twelve Steps for recovery. It had worked for them and it could work for us.

Many of us looked at the Twelve Steps in their entirety and felt overwhelmed with panic and paralysis; we avoided them until it was clear that we needed to take action and risks. Slowly, we became aware that we, too, could rid ourselves of anger, bitterness and resentment and apply the principles of the program to our lives.

Some experienced a rush of change after taking the first Three Steps. Suddenly, responsibilities were reduced to manageable propor-

tions and we started to see the world differently—to trust again, to feel gratitude and to detach
with love from the alcoholic. This level of spiritual growth was enough until we became conscious of the need for changes in ourselves.
When the need became compelling, we started to
move on, taking Steps Four through Seven. We
began to experience freedom and happiness
which we had never dreamed possible.

Members often found a period of complacency
again before finding it necessary to work the
Eighth and Ninth Steps. But the process of making amends to those we had harmed brought our
housekeeping chores up-to-date.

Taking Step Ten allowed us to prevent the negative emotions from regaining their foothold. By
taking a daily inventory, we rid ourselves of the
"little" problems which past experience has
taught us have the potential to become insur-
mountable crises. We became ready for Steps
Eleven and Twelve.

Most Al-Anon members have found it easier
to work the Steps with a sponsor. The caring and

empathy of one who has been down the path ahead of us gives us the faith that we, too, can overcome our fears. The hope of this program is that no matter where we have been, no matter where we are, no matter how much we hurt, our lives can be transformed and our spirits can be healed.

First, I found I could stop my negative thinking and replace it with positive thoughts, but only while at a meeting. Then slowly as I began to accept myself, with my limitations and my capabilities, I regained faith in myself. I was then able to move on with my own personal growth and keep fears and apprehension under control for a few hours beyond the meeting, until eventually a whole day was under control. My faith in myself continued to grow as a result; I had faith in my husband. And this terrible wall of ice that had encompassed me for so long began to melt, and I accepted the fact that he was a sick person and I did love him. Communication slowly returned, nurtured by constant Al-Anon meetings.

—*Australia*

In Al-Anon, I have learned that my perception of my life can determine how I feel about my situation. If I am feeling full of self-pity, this is how my world looks: We live in the country, so far away from everything. It is so hard to get to Al-Anon meetings. I can't talk on the telephone because it costs so much and we're on the manual exchange, so the operators can listen in. It gets so lonely at night because my husband's job takes him away from home so much. He leaves me to look after our small farm as well as doing my own housework, and it is so much extra, exhausting work. You can bet if anything is going to go wrong, it will happen when he is away The children catch a bus to school, leaving early and getting home late, so I am alone for hours at a time. At the moment, my car is in the garage, getting a new motor, so I am stuck here. I can't even go shopping or pick up the mail.

My husband is in AA, but there are still problems. Life should be better with him sober; we should have more money, but I still have to make my own bread. Everyone keeps telling me to keep coming to Al Anon and things will improve, but they haven't had to put up with my problems.

If I feel full of gratitude, I look at the same situation in a different way: We live in the country. It is so beautiful to have nature and all her glories around me every day. The distance makes it a bit harder to get to Al-Anon meetings, but I can always read Al-Anon literature. It doesn't cost that much to call another member for three minutes; the girls on the manual exchange might listen in, but they can only learn something good.

My husband's job takes him away from home a lot, but I accept this. It gives me a chance to spend more time with the children and to do the things he doesn't care for, like reading in bed or listening to the radio. Not being one to relish housework much, it is great for me to be able to get out among the animals, to feed and care for them and get loving trust in return. My work inside the house eventually gets done; if not today, it won't run away. If anything goes wrong, we have wonderful neighbors who are only too pleased to come and help. The children catch a bus to school, going early and getting home late, leaving me to enjoy the peace that solitude and a good relationship with God, as I understand Him, can bring. My car is in the garage at the moment getting a new motor. This means I am grounded for a few days, but I have an excellent chance to catch up on the ironing and other things I need to do. One of my neighbors took me shopping with her yesterday; and we enjoyed each other's company.

I nearly forgot: My husband is sober in AA. How lovely it is not to have a drunk around the house. We share the program with each other and with the children, who are in Alateen. It hasn't always been easy, but we have learned so much good from the program. I have a batch of bread in the oven and the smell pervading my kitchen is beautiful.

All in all, my life is pretty good. We have a few problems which we prefer to call situations because situations have a habit of changing. Al-Anon has done wonders for me.

—*Australia*

The days I choose to live negatively really are not too much fun. Even having the right to that choice is a freedom I have never allowed myself. I put a time limit on it. Negative living dampens my soul, and I like sunlight. It is hard to see God's beauty in the dark, whether it be in me, my family, friends, strangers, or in the unlimited creations of nature around me.

—*Venezuela*

When I came to my first meeting, I knew that I was powerless over alcohol. What I hadn't realized was that almost every area of my life had become unmanageable: I had no friends; my house was a wreck; I had made no progress in my career for ten years due to numerous "geographical cures"; I had difficulty making decisions; I was depressed all the time; and even though I was only in my early thirties, I felt that the most interesting and enjoyable of life's activities were behind me. I had no ambition because I had no hope of any changes.

After almost six years in Al-Anon, I have deeply fulfilling friendships, my career is back on track and, although my house wouldn't receive a gold star from the health department, it is usually habitable. I very seldom experience mood swings and I let my Higher Power help me with major decisions. I can truly say that my life has become manageable.

—*Anonymous*

Before Al-Anon, I lived tied to the alcoholic. I was always aware of what he did or said, my thoughts and my feelings were a real mess. I could not control my attitude toward other people; I didn't know how to love, how to think, and I couldn't make decisions. I let myself be controlled by events, so I had become a slave to other people's actions.

I didn't know where I was going; I didn't have a goal; I was simply there. Today, I know that my goal is freedom. Today, I can laugh even if somebody else is sad or angry. I am convinced that

37

each human being is free to choose a role in the theater of life. If somebody else chooses the role of musician and plays a waltz, it is up to me to dance or not. Similarly, I am free to choose what I want to do with my life: how to think, to love or hate, be happy or sad.

Today, I have also learned that being free is to allow those I love the choice of how to think, to feel, to act, to dress, to eat, to be wrong, to be angry—and to live without getting angry at them for expressing themselves. I will respect their points of view, even when they are not in agreement with mine, because I have learned that all are free to live their own lives. It is wonderful to be able to feel this freedom that God has given me through the program, most of all because I know that I am totally free to follow it or not.
—*Mexico*

In learning to forgive myself, it helps me to recognize that there were times I did not know I had a choice, just as the alcoholic may not know he has a choice to drink or stay sober. Today I am thinking with a clearer mind; I am learning to release the choices that I thought were mine to make which really belong to someone else. In other words, I am learning to mind my own business.

—*Louisiana, United States*

A stumbling block in my learning to accept the First Step was a statement that I made when I was about twelve years old. I was angry at my mother for putting up with my dad's drinking and for always making up with him after a bad incident. I once said to my mother, "I'll never marry a man who drinks." Her response was, "You just wait and see. You'll find out what you have to put up with after you're married." I became even more determined to stick to my conviction.

I came into Al-Anon twenty years later and heard the "Suggested Welcome": ". . . It is possible for us to find contentment and even happiness whether the alcoholic is still drinking or not."

That made me angry. How could I find happiness and contentment when he was out drinking and I was stuck at home with three children?

The Welcome also said a change in attitude is a help to the alcoholic. I didn't want to hear this either. Why should I be the one to change? But this is what I had to learn if I wanted happiness and contentment.

I thought that accepting a situation meant I had to like it or that I would be giving in to something that I had said I wouldn't put up with. My spiritual awakening on the First Step occurred when my family went on a two week vacation to the East Coast. I dreaded the trip, but my family was going with our without me, so I went. How could I face everyone and explain to them that the reason I really didn't want to go was because of my husband's drinking problem?

Crossing the Mississippi River, I made up my mind that I was going to have a good time, regardless of my husband's behavior. A beautiful feeling came over me and I had no control over it. I felt at peace with myself. I remember looking at my husband and feeling love and compassion for him. The trip turned out to be a most memorable experience because I had let go of the controlling reins and I had accepted him just as he was.

There came a change in my attitude and our relationship improved even though he continued to drink. I had the feeling that now there was truly hope for me. I could go on to Step Two and believe that God could restore me to sanity. I had accepted the First Step in my heart.

—*Missouri, United States*

I started slowly to understand that I could no longer be God. The job was much too hard and the hours too long. Whenever I had tried to change people or things and failed, I lost more of my self-esteem. In order to get out of this job, I had to let go.

—*Massachusetts, United States*

My life was truly unmanageable. The job of trying to manage the lives of those around me built resentment, self-pity, despair and all the other negative emotions that made me sick and harmed those around me.

Finally the fog started to lift. The Al-Anon message was to let go of the people I loved and stop trying to manage their lives; I couldn't even manage my own. I learned the difference between submission and surrender. As I tried to turn my will and my life over to the care of God as I understood Him, I saw the benefits I received in exchange for my self-will.

The greatest benefit was my own mental health. The second was a husband who loved me and wanted to share the responsibilities I had carried so long. He gives me emotional and financial support and helps raise our daughter.

Giving others their freedom has given me my own. I have been given a partner instead of a child, and I can be a partner instead of a manager. I have been given love and respect. I can ask for help when I need it. I don't have to do it all myself anymore. I have found the ability to back off when I can't solve a problem, and I can put it in God's hands. I have learned I don't have to be above or below anyone else. I can feel gratitude and compassion. I now know love, the kind of love that does not possess, but waits and listens.

—*Ohio, United States*

I really made a decision to turn my will and my life over to the care of God as I understood Him, and began to pray for knowledge of His will for me rather than a list of things I thought were my due after years of hardship and misery. It was only then that I began to feel the serenity and courage mentioned in the Serenity Prayer.

Even though the problems in our home multiplied as my husband's alcoholism progressed, I really had come to believe that a Power greater than myself could restore me to sanity. Each time I felt I had reached the limit of my endurance and told my Higher Power, "That's it! I'm at the end of my tether!", relief came. Either the general situation improved, or I suddenly found myself with a new surge of courage and serenity. At first, I was overwhelmed by what seemed a miracle, but gradually it dawned on me that this was what the Al-Anon program and philosophy were all about.

Instead of questioning why things happened as they did, I was able to accept them as part of my destiny, as an opportunity for growth offered by my Higher Power. I still have the will to decide what I will do about them, and with the help of the Al-Anon program and its world-wide fellowship, I often make the right decision.

—*Anonymous*

The process of turning our life and will over to the care of God in Step Three begins by working the rest of the Steps and it involves more than giving up our defects. It involves giving God our assets, too.

Some of my most significant growth has come

from asking Him to use and improve both defects and assets. When I think I am totally honest, there is no room for improvement. But when I give Him that quality, I begin to be more honest about myself. I can admit my defects to another person instead of squelching them. A totally honest person who is afraid to let anyone know his inadequacies is caught in a dreadful dilemma; fear and guilt feed each other. So when I give my honesty to God, I may open up a wound of character defects, but I will drain off guilt and I will experience the freedom that comes with being healed.

Have you ever felt guilty about admitting your good points because they're not perfect or you haven't used them recently? The thought of God cleaning up my assets for His use is exciting. Once, when I was having trouble making amends through an attitude (and therefore a behavior) change, I kept giving God the defect which I thought was causing the trouble only to find myself holding onto another one. Finally, I decided to give Him my asset of acceptance and

I was given the freedom of accepting the other person and myself exactly the way we were that day. Such relief! The irony is that three months later, this person made amends to me and today we are friends. The principle works every time I use it.

—*Texas, United States*

In Step One, I surrendered. I admitted I had failed to control the drinking and that everything in my life was miserable and unmanageable. In surrendering and in coming to Al-Anon, I was showing that I was ready for help. I wanted to feel and to look like the well members I saw at meetings.

In Step Two, I began to see hope. A Power outside myself could restore me to sanity and lead me to peace and happiness. At first, this power was the group, my sponsor and the love of individual members. I began to realize that this Power is an all-powerful, guiding, creative, intelligent force that isn't fixed in one or two people or just in my group. This Power pervades every group and was even willing to dwell in me at times. I learned to trust that somehow the Power would come to me when I needed it: through meetings that touch me, through people, through reading Al-Anon literature and through the enlightenment of looking at old problems a new way. I choose to call this Power "God." After concluding that God exists and is there to help me every day, I was ready for Step Three, to find a God of my understanding.

It's the God of my understanding that made this Step so difficult for me. My understanding of God was very limited. I had not grown in understanding God as rapidly as I had grown in years. He remained the God I had learned about in my childhood—a God that could do miracles centuries ago, a God that got very angry with people like me, and a God who dwelt up high in Heaven and was far removed from me and my personal struggles. Yet these people in Al-Anon and the program itself assured me that this wasn't all there was to God. He had every right to be sad about how I conducted my life, but He loved me and was willing to help me become the beautiful person He had created me to be. He only needed me to ask Him to come into my life for He wasn't a pushy God. He was gentle and patient and understood human frailty. So, with just enough faith to hope this was what God wanted, I made a once-and-for-all decision to turn my will and my life over to His care. I chuckle to myself now when I think of that day and my once-and-for-all decision. I had invited God to come into my life but I had no idea how I thought things should be or how often I would close the door to God and let my will run wild. But with each struggle I have with God, I learn more about His beauty, love and patience. He isn't so far removed from me now. He's become my best friend. I still say, "No God, this time I think you're wrong. I won't." And God waits until my whole being realizes that I'm incapable of doing it alone, that His way is the best way. He has miraculously given me the strength and courage to face life as it is. I have His help and guidance to weather the storms and to enjoy the beauty I had not seen before.

—*Manitoba, Canada*

Throughout the Al-Anon literature runs the message, "We tried it this way and it worked for us." I had to decide whether I wanted to try it the way it worked or continue on my own way, which wasn't working. This was the first freedom I encountered, the freedom of choice.

I began working the Steps after a period of suspicion and mistrust. Step One gave me the freedom to stop controlling. It showed me that I was powerless over alcohol and the alcoholic, and with that freedom I was able to concentrate on my life, which had certainly become unmanageable.

Step Two gave me a belief in a power greater than myself and the freedom to think rationally. My thoughts no longer raced around in my head like a dog chasing its tail.

Step Three seemed like a trap. It was okay to

believe in a Higher Power, but Step Three required me to turn my will and my life over to the care of God as I understood Him. What would happen? I was gaining a bit of freedom and would have to give it up. If I took this Step, He could now use me. The price I was going to have to pay was the freedom of my self-will. Was it worth it? So I procrastinated. But then I read again: "We tried it this way and it worked for us."

Talents I didn't know existed in me were allowed to surface. Companionship, giving and receiving love, communication, freedom from fear and guilt, and freedom from the shackles of somebody else's alcoholism were all given to me as a result of the first Three Steps. These freedoms were beyond my wildest dreams.

—New Zealand

Coming to believe that alcoholism was an illness was easy, but accepting my powerlessness over anything that affected the man I loved was far from easy. I wanted to believe that I had not caused this illness, so I accepted this with ease, but I hung on tenaciously to the thought that there had to be something I could do about it. It was pointed out to me by older members that a change in attitude might help. To change my attitude, I had to change myself. Finally, I was forced to take the Fourth Step. Taking an inventory as the Step suggested was a tremendous shock to my inflated ego. I found that I could no longer live with myself and continue to be complacent and self-righteous about my character defects and mistakes in the past. I had to accept these without trying to justify them, do what I could about them and leave them in the past. With this came the realization and acceptance of the fact that I am the only person I can change and I cannot alter many situations. Accepting this brought relief. This knowledge made me aware of who and what I was responsible for. It gave me the time I needed to make the changes in myself that I knew were necessary.

—*Louisiana, United States*

51

I came to Al-Anon a crusty shell of bitterness, loneliness and despair. I looked around the room at the first meeting—at the slogans, the Steps and the Serenity Prayer, and curled my lips inside. This was another one of the "religious" places, and I was plenty mad at God—if there even was one.

But something from way back in the depths of my mind groped toward the peace in that room, because after the meeting I asked for some literature. The only thing there that night was a booklet about the Fourth Step inventory. Later as I thumbed through it, I found a half-empty page on which it said to list my assets and liabilities, so I picked up a pen and started to itemize. At the top on the liability list I wrote, "too cynical."

Some months later as I talked with an embittered newcomer, my insides lurched. "I'm not like that anymore! I'm not a cynic! I am able to listen with an open mind and heart. How did you do that, God? I didn't even believe in you then."

I didn't have to make any big pronouncements—no ceremonies—didn't even have to believe. All I had to do was become just the least bit willing to open my clutched fist, a tiny, grudging bit, and miracles happened. That's God as I understand Him today.

—*Texas, United States*

As I was growing up, I was always taught to be kind and considerate of other people. I was very compliant and I developed into a "people-pleaser," always eager to act in ways which gained the approval of those around me. When I found myself married to an alcoholic, there was nothing I could do to please him. He demanded my complete devotion; slowly the other relationships in my life deteriorated. We tried several "geographical cures." This further eroded relationships with family and friends. By the time I found Al-Anon, I had almost no support system left and I had given up trying to make friends.

While taking my Fourth Step inventory, I learned that I had ignored the people I loved the most in my effort to meet the impossibly high expectations of the alcoholic. Had I directed some of that loving attention to healthy people around me, I would have received love and encouragement from them. By keeping silent about the problem, I gave them no opportunity to help me. And sadly, I missed many opportunities to love and support them.

In Al-Anon, I learned to tell people that I loved, needed and appreciated them. In return, I have received bountiful expressions of love and support, even when I don't need them. What a blessing!

—*Ohio, United States*

While giving away my Fifth Step, I realized that I had always expected perfection of myself. Since I considered myself a good person, I suffered greatly when I noticed shortcomings in myself. And true to my obsessive personality, I had agonized over each mistake, repeatedly. I found it revealing that I had a very difficult time recalling pleasant events in my life, but I could remember embarrassments, humiliations, oversights and depressions in vivid detail. My sponsor helped me realize that I had blown these incidents out of proportion and that my recent involvement with an alcoholic and my consequent withdrawal and depression were normal responses to the circumstances. This helped me to relieve my guilt and focus on positive events and decisions in my life.

—*Anonymous*

When our spiritual lives feel strained, we needn't pound ourselves relentlessly. With spiritual insight, we can find out where our greatest strengths and weaknesses lie, and can acknowledge our weaknesses as something good and meaningful. This gives us a feeling of strength, belief, and open-mindedness, a more fulfilling way of life, and a greater sense of gratitude.

—*Anonymous*

It is in fellowship with others and in human relationships that we grow, but it is often so painful. My goal must be to work on my defects for my own peace of mind, asking God's help and accepting that I will often fail, which is a good lesson in humility.

—*New Hampshire, United States*

I had been a shocking liar and I had been consumed by a bitter hatred towards certain people for years. This soured my whole life. My days were taken up planning revenge, and the fact that I never put any of these crazy plans into action was due more to cowardice than to good nature. My rotten thinking and my contempt for myself because of this all but completely destroyed me.

Deep down I had the nagging knowledge that there would be no real relief from myself until I could bring my problem into the open and talk to somebody else about it, and after some time wrestling with myself, I became willing to do so. There I left it, for I believe that if we are willing, the time, the place and the right person will be provided for us, and this is just what happened. A minister of religion happened to come to my home for something or other, and I just found myself talking to him. Relief flowed in as the nastiness was talked out. When I became sufficiently honest and sufficiently humble to do the Fifth Step, I added a spiritual experience to my spiritual beliefs and by doing so, gained courage and strength and the beginnings of the peace of mind I had longed for.

—*New Zealand*

For me, the most devastating effect of my husband's alcoholism was that I became increasingly isolated from family and friends. A series of moves took us farther and farther from my family, and each time we moved to a new community, it was more difficult to reach out and make friends. So when it came time for me to make a list of persons I had harmed, I realized that I hadn't interacted with many people and the list was very short. My main sins were sins of omission. When my father was dying, I was unable to tell him how much I loved him; I could only feel the loss and keep it inside. I was unable to offer solace to my mother at the time because my own needs were overwhelming. But the biggest omission was failing to take care of myself. I just didn't have the energy.

So I made amends to myself. I forgave myself for forgetting to enjoy God's blessings. I forgave myself for acting as if I were being held hostage. I forgave myself for dwelling in despair and self-pity. And I forgave myself for not recognizing that the man I married was headed into alcoholism until the disease had caused irreparable harm to our relationship. Then I was able to make amends to others. I could renew communications with friends and relatives I had neglected for years. And the relief was wonderful. I was welcomed with open arms, and no one sought any explanations for my negligence. They loved me just as I was. Of course, my outlook and attitudes had vastly improved after many, many Al-Anon meetings.

Finally, God offered me another chance to console my mother. She had remarried a few years after my father died. And soon it became clear that my stepfather's death was inevitable. During the final weeks of his life and during the funeral preparations, I was able to help and comfort my mother and share love instead of fear and self-pity, and I didn't need to add anything to my burden of guilt.

—Ohio, United States

My sponsor suggested that I make amends to myself for all the rough treatment I had subjected myself to during the years of illness. At first, I thought it was a peculiar idea, but then I realized that it was the next logical step in taking responsibility for my attitudes, emotions and actions. This awareness came during a meeting as I listened to a newcomer agonize over her decision to post a property bond to get her son out of jail. She was using a lot of phrases like,

"He has caused so many problems," and "He has divided our family." I could see that she was choosing to worry and I could almost feel her anxiety, but she clearly knew no other way to react. She felt responsible for his disease and his actions, so she was taking responsibility which was rightfully his because she knew no other alternative.

It became clear to me that I had spent endless hours in self-imposed anxiety states worrying about the alcoholic in my life. I had succeeded only in giving myself migraine headaches, depression, and frustration. Worrying and agonizing had never changed anything. Looking back, I can see that I knew no other coping mechanisms. I did not know how to relieve the stress or distinguish my responsibilities from the alcoholic's responsibilities. I worried continually and I felt anxious if I didn't have anything specific to worry about. I lived in a constant state of dread, expecting catastrophes and crises. When they occurred, I blamed myself for not being able to prevent them.

Now, I see that I used the only coping mechanisms I knew. I have forgiven myself for causing myself all those years of pain. I know that I did the best I could under the circumstances, but even better, I know that I will never have to live that way again.

—*Anonymous*

In thinking of the personalities of my four children, one always stood out: my little rebel, my oldest daughter, my second child. During her childhood, I rarely tried to analyze my children's similarities or differences or my daughter's rebelliousness. Now, as I think of it, many things might have contributed to it: moving in with my husband's family for economic reasons during the Depression years, the confusion of an alcoholic situation, or too many demands from too many adults. But, it wasn't until many years later that it came to light.

My daughter had her own home, and her children were out of college and had careers in other

61

cities. During one of my visits to her home, she told me a story that happened many years before at a children's home. A little boy had run away from home, and when they found him, he struck out at them in rebellion. This was the only way he knew to get the love he needed.

Almost immediately, I had a flashback to my daughter's childhood. When she would yell at me, I would yell back even louder, striking her instead of taking her into my arms and loving her. As so often happens in an alcoholic home, I was taking my fear out on her. In my mind, I could see it so clearly. She had been reaching out for love and I had denied her.

In a moment, we were in each other's arms, loving and crying to make up for all the years of reaching out for love. A great healing emotion for both of us ensued, as God forgave us both.

Since that night, we have been able to share so much in our new relationship. The peace that comes with forgiveness is the serenity we learn in Al-Anon. My ten years with sobriety and

Al-Anon have taught me to love, and that love is healing. Without my Al-Anon tools, I might not have realized or recognized my daughter's reaching out for love.

—Florida, United States

Making amends isn't just saying, "I'm sorry." It means responding differently from our new understanding.

—New Jersey, United States

I have learned that today I am a composite of every experience I have ever had, the good ones and the bad ones. So I can forgive myself the mistakes of the past. I have become able to see myself in my proper perspective with God and my fellow man. I have learned not only to know my limitations but to know and have respect for my capabilities. I can accept praise or criticism from you because you love me for what I am and I feel worthy of your love. Once I did not. I have learned to live One Day at a Time, asking for knowledge of God's will for me each day and the power to carry it out, knowing that I must accept whatever comes as His will and knowing that somehow it is best for me.

—*Louisiana, United States*

Autumn is a time for harvest. As I picked the last of the cucumbers and discovered a few peppers among the weeds, I thought how much more abundant my crop of vegetables might have been had I done more weeding, more cultivating. But I'd been sick for a month this summer and the weeds had really gotten ahead of me. The herb garden had almost disappeared. The only way to keep a herb border neat is to work on it for just a few minutes each day, pulling up weeds that poke up, unwanted and unwelcome.

Bending over, the sun warm on my back, I found myself thinking that weeding a garden was similar in a lot of ways to taking the Tenth Step. No matter how honest our taking of the Fourth, Fifth, Sixth and Seventh Steps, there's no guarantee that we won't find ourselves growing a new crop of the uglies that have to be weeded out. Using the Tenth Step—and using it often—can uncover a defect before it becomes firmly rooted.

As I yanked and pulled and dug out crabgrass, I thought how much easier it would have been to remove all those weeds when they were tiny. Character defects, too, have a way of taking hold unless uprooted early.

Sometimes, a swift, small, uncomfortable feeling tells me I've been wrong, and before I can continue to grow straight and tall, I must promptly admit it. I like to take a personal inventory in the late afternoon. That way, there's only an evening to quickly review at bedtime, if I'm not too sleepy. Also, I've found it convenient to use the *Blueprint for Progress: Al-Anon's Fourth Step Inventory* booklet, not only to dig out the weeds, but to gather a few complimentary bouquets!

— Connecticut, United States

Layers and layers of bitterness, self-punishing guilt, self-righteousness and self-loathing were slowly and painfully peeled off and a person began to emerge. I've heard people in Al-Anon say they got back their self-worth. I had never had any in my life, so it was a whole new feeling to like the person called "me."

—*Massachusetts, United States*

When I look at myself now, I can hardly believe I am the same person. I feel enthusiastic, self-directed, and happy most of the time. I am so busy that I scarcely have enough time to do all the things I'd like to be doing.

—*Illinois, United States*

I started telling my children I was grateful for little things they said or did. I reminded myself to be grateful for finishing a task and doing it well. The more I spoke about gratitude, the more I became aware of things to be grateful for. I prayed about it and my Higher Power began opening my eyes. I would lie in bed at night and say the alphabet, counting all the things I had to be grateful for, starting with the letter A. My attitude began to change. I started learning that I had a lot to be grateful for, and I began to feel grateful.

This made a great change in my life. I started to have a sense of well-being. I began reaching out to others to share my abundance. I let go of my need to please others and to meet their expectations. I started saying a little prayer and following my heart.

This new attitude of gratitude is a part of me. It is not just a burst of emotion, untamed and sporadic. It is a quiet, daily reality that goes with me into every situation. I still have off-days, but with my Higher Power and my program, it all works out.

—Manitoba, Canada

Al-Anon has taught me that change is possible, in fact, inevitable, so that I don't have to be mired in unhappiness when things go badly, or regret that something is gone when I lose someone or something I love. A new beauty, a new life, will spring out of everything that happens if I keep practicing the Twelve Steps and learn to live joyfully, acceptingly, One Day at a Time.

—*New Hampshire, United States*

3

Concepts of a
Higher Power

As Al-Anon members, we are encouraged to
define spiritual concepts in our own terms and
are free to arrive at our own spiritual truths. On
our journey toward a spiritual awakening we are
given the experience set down in Step Two.
Others, before us, came to believe in a Power
greater than themselves, a Higher Power that
could restore them to sanity. Some may feel
unsure about the nature of this Power. They are

comfortable using the experience and strength of the group as their definition, while others come into the fellowship with firm convictions. Still others may express doubt that spiritual forces exist. What ever our beliefs, we do not force them on others.

The importance of defining that Higher Power becomes clear in Step Three. We "made a decision to turn our will and our lives over to the care of God *as we understood Him*."

An Al-Anon member from California explained: "I want to work out my own ideas about a God of my understanding rather than to submit to someone else's interpretation about what and what not to believe. After all, Al-Anon has shown me to think for myself. Only in that way can I be comfortable in my belief. From the slogan, Live and Let Live, I learned to respect others' beliefs and feelings as well as my own; therefore, if I urged my beliefs on someone else, it would be self-defeating. Would this be following the Al-Anon program? Would this be practicing the principles in all my affairs? We are all different individuals with differing backgrounds. How can I possibly think that my thoughts and beliefs are what another person needs or wants? All of us are trying to improve our 'conscious contact' as it says in the Eleventh Step."

In Al-Anon, we can come to understand the nature of a Power greater than ourselves in a personal, profound way and many of us have been amazed at the difference this understanding makes in our lives. We know if we pursue our truths with sincere humility and honesty we will find them.

The members sharing in this chapter are expressing very personal concepts of the spiritual forces that they believe have restored them to sanity. They have shared their definitions and each of us is free to accept these, substitute our own, or reject them altogether.

I grew up obediently. My parents expected me to go to church, so I went. I never understood much about my religion, and when I left home, I gradually stopped attending. I would go back for a holiday or a wedding, but I categorized these as ritual occasions, not religious events.

After several years with no religious involvement and very little exposure to religious people, I found myself in an Al-Anon meeting with people who were openly crediting their Higher Power with transforming their lives. I didn't know what to think about their ideas. I had always considered myself well-versed in religious matters, but I had never heard people speak of a power that had a direct effect on their circumstances. I felt a little alienated from the group, but they had some indefinable something that I wanted, so I tried just being open to what they had to say.

One day, I was discussing some of my doubts with a minister and he asked me if I thought God loved me and I said: "Well, it depends what day you ask me." And he said, "Yes, I know what you mean." He really helped me to understand that even if I only have glimpses of my Higher Power's effect on my life, it is still more than I had before. I can marvel at the coincidences, express my gratitude, and practice the Al-Anon Steps. My Higher Power will guide me and provide for my needs. All I have to do is continue to be open and work on living each day well.

—*Wisconsin, United States*

I arrived at my first Al-Anon meeting emotionally hurting, mentally bewildered, and spiritually numb. Gradually, the love and laughter I found at my meetings penetrated my shell and brought me out of my self-imposed isolation. Little by little, I began to work the program and soon came to realize the importance of the Eleventh Step. Every time I had a decision to make, I would ask for God's guidance and then sit back and wonder what the answer was supposed to be. "Just give me a sign for what direction I must take," I would pray. "Any burning bush will do."

This became an increasingly worrisome problem for me after several months in the program. A new-found honesty forced me to evaluate my marriage, and I came to the painful conclusion that there were too many problems—some that involved drinking and some that did not—and that perhaps the best solution would be for us to separate. Although I know now that this was the best thing I could have done for myself, at the time I was buried in guilt. The only single people I knew in Al-Anon then were those who had never been married. The ones who were married had lasting marriages, and I guess I had come to equate staying married with working a good program. At meetings, I had talked often about how important it was to me to learn God s will for my life. How could a separation or a divorce be God's will? Didn't God want people to stay married? I felt as though I had failed Al-Anon when I finally did leave my husband.

About that time, I was fortunate enough to attend an Al-Anon conference with my sponsor. The lovely woman who opened the meeting told us how wonderful Al-Anon had been for her and how grateful she was for the beautiful life she was now able to live. I sat huddled against the wall, unable to reconcile the feeling that a divorce was now my best answer with the contrary conviction that it couldn't possibly be God's will and was therefore proof positive that I was not working a good program. The woman concluded, "I know I shall always continue with this joyous, beautiful way of life, even though I divorced my alcoholic husband twenty years ago." I was stunned. The next speaker talked about her divorce of two years earlier and how she had been helped by the loving support of her group. Some of the other speakers also shared their experiences with divorce and separation while in Al-Anon.

Gradually, I realized that I was receiving a message from my Higher Power through this meeting. He was not telling me to get a divorce, but neither was He telling me to remain in a marriage that had died years ago. He was telling me that whatever I decided to do, He loved me enough to be with me, and that He would use my choice for His greater good, if I would only place this choice and its results in His hands.

This may seem so simple that it does not even bear mentioning, but it was quite a revelation to me that one had to take the Third Step before the Eleventh Step. Of course, I believed that I had taken the Third Step, but all I had done was to accept intellectually that "placing my will and my life" in His care would be a good thing to do. In other words, I had made a decision to make a decision, and had blithely gone on my merry way. This was what was jeopardizing the quality of my program, although I mistakenly thought my problems came from not being able to figure out God's will.

The difficulty I was having with "praying only for knowledge of His will" was that I had pictured His will as a straight and narrow path and believed that I was in trouble if I ever deviated from this line. Since I was never sure I was on the right path to begin with, it's easy to see how confused I would get and why I was always looking for a sign. Yet, saying that only one direction in life represents God's will is like saying there is only one right and proper route to take between two cities and heaven help you if you take a wrong road along the way. In reality, there are many routes to choose from, both on the highway and in our lives, and God is willing to work with our choices, if we will only let Him.

Had I joined Al-Anon earlier, I am sure that God would have taken that choice and used it to make my life beautiful. Instead, I stubbornly held onto my problems working them out on my own, or so I thought, until I finally had to admit my powerlessness. Then God took that choice and made my life just as beautiful as He would have if I had begun the Steps years earlier. You see, I feel that my Higher Power isn't one particular route in life. To me, He is the whole road map. Now, I ask God's guidance as I travel.

He helps me to know I am a good person. One step at a time He is healing me, by helping me to release old resentments, old hurts, and old fears. He is showing me that I am a much stronger person than I thought.

Illinois, United States

I really wanted to use the Steps in my Al-Anon recovery, but since I am an atheist, I did not think it was possible. Attending meetings without working the Steps, however, was not giving me what I needed. I finally decided to rely on the experiences of others as my Higher Power. After years of being self-reliant, it felt good to try to benefit from what others had learned.

I began to seek out the experiences of other people in Al-Anon who seemed to be living serenely. I asked them how they managed to survive through the difficult situations they faced. I was not content to have what I considered to be easy answers thrown back at me. I tried not to be hostile, but I wanted to know how they talked to themselves, how they managed to get out of bed in the morning and how they kept going in the face of adversity. I asked them what pieces of Al-Anon literature would help me. I read it and studied it and tried to apply it to my life. Soon, I came to believe that their experiences could restore me to sanity. That is how I did Step Two.

Step Three was more difficult and it took me longer to come to terms with it, but I came to believe that if I put into practice all that I had learned in Step Two, I would stop repeating my old mistakes. By learning from the experiences of others, I could change my behavior and attitudes. Soon, I felt a new sense of security that I had never had before. I felt confident. I believed that my life was in the care of a Higher Power.

In Steps Five, Six and Seven, I learned to be honest and to accept myself the way I was. I learned that although I am human, I could improve. This was new for me because I never thought I could change. Before Al-Anon, I accepted myself with reservations because I had no hope of change. Now, I accept myself without reservation because I know that I am trying my best every day. This has been true for others in my group and I have no reason to believe it won't be true for me.

I learned to pray and meditate. I direct prayer inward and meditate on self-improvement since I am unable to conceive of a Higher Power—out there. Instead of trying to solve everyone else's problems, I spend my time honestly examining my thoughts, motives and actions each day. This approach to the Steps has helped me feel serene and optimistic for the first time in my life. Someday, I may have a different idea of a Higher Power, but for today, I am satisfied with my ability to apply the experiences of others to my own situation.

—*Anonymous*

I had no belief in a Higher Power when I came into the Al-Anon program. Slowly, I began to trust the people in my group and finally began to use the group as my Higher Power. Several months later, I wanted to find God, but didn't know how. I felt I couldn't find Him in a church.

I had looked there as a child, but never found love.

One week, a guest led a Third Step meeting. By the way he talked, I knew that he knew God and had a personal relationship with Him. After the meeting, I asked him how I could find this God. He answered, "Say 'Good Morning, God,' every morning even if you don't believe it."

I thought it was too simple, but I was desperate, so I tried it every morning for about two months and one morning when I said it, I knew there was a God. I knew He heard me and He loved me.

—New York, United States

The God I grew up learning about was strict and demanding and measured people by impossible standards. My understanding of that God wasn't restoring me to sanity; it was driving me crazy. I wanted to find what kind of Higher Power was working in the lives of the people I met in Al-Anon. All I was asked to do was to

Keep Coming Back. No one asked for money I didn't have or time I didn't have or words I didn't have. I came and listened to their experience, strength and hope.

There were rough times because of my tendency to put certain people on a pedestal. I would expect impossible standards from them and then would be disappointed because they were human. It was unfair of me to make such demands of other people. My only hope for survival would be my belief in a spiritual power.

I felt that getting rid of the disrupting influences in my life (anger, self-pity, hate, resentment) would make room for hope and faith to grow. I am coming to believe that my God has not changed, but my understanding of Him has changed through Al-Anon.

—*Manitoba, Canada*

I grew up in an Orthodox home where the God of my understanding was comforting, and His teachings provided an answer for everything.

When I was ten, however, my father died, and the God of my understanding died with him. Throughout my adolescence, I had no belief in God or religion. When I thought of either, anger welled up inside me.

Then I met and married my husband. Once again, all seemed right with the world until alcoholism reared its ugly head. I felt deserted once again. If I had been angry with God before, I was furious now.

I began attending Al-Anon meetings and trying to find a God and a faith that I could live with. Others there seemed to have something I was lacking in my life. I attended churches of several denominations, seeking that elusive "something" I perceived in them.

As part of this quest, I attended an Al-Anon spiritual weekend. After the close of the Al-Anon meeting, I decided to join in an outdoor communion service. I arrived a bit late. It was a magnificent spring day and looking through the doors, I could see sunshine glistening on the heads of those who attended. Surrounding them were the signs of their faith; a minister in his white robe, a simple wooden cross. I strained to open the massive glass door, but it seemed stuck.

Suddenly, I felt a warmth on my shoulder and a voice whispered to me using my biblical name, "You don't belong there." I stood motionless as a feeling of love and peace washed over me. My childhood faith had been restored. I had always felt like an outsider but as I looked at the Al-Anon members I had shared so much with, I felt closer to them then ever.

—New Jersey, United States

Through the program, I learned that my attitudes needed housecleaning. I was blocking myself from God's love because I had not forgiven myself. I learned that God speaks to me through my feelings, my thoughts, books I read, and wonder of wonders, through people. My concept of God changed as I allowed people to get close to me, as I was able to share my pain, and as I was able to rid myself of resentments and anger by doing Steps Four and Five.

I came to understand how important it is that I believe in myself, to trust my feelings and judgments, to recognize my abilities, and most of all, to make my own decisions. I learned that I can only do my best to live the way God wants me to live, One Day at a Time, and then let Him help me with the rest.

—*Manitoba, Canada*

"Oh, my God." How often I've used that phrase. We learn it as children and it stays with us forever, so it seems. We call upon Him for everything, big or small, consciously or unconsciously.

I became aware of Him at a very early age, even prior to school. I'd hear, "Don't do that; God will punish you." Looking back, that's about when I started to close my mind to religion. Bring me to church, I'd fall asleep. Send me to instruction classes, I'd get there late, get "sick," and leave early. There was no way I was going to hang around and get blamed and punished for something I hadn't done.

"Hell-fire and brimstone" were phrases I remember from that period. My fears started early and continued on. Being raised in an alcoholic home, there was no one to talk to. God was out, that was for sure. Talking to Him could only bring on more troubles. I learned detachment at a very early age; He was the first to go.

Twenty-five years later, I attended my first Al-Anon meeting. Someone told me, "Let Go and Let God." Oh, oh. Wrong place. He's *here*, too, and who needs this? Not me. A friend comforted me by telling me to listen for other things. "Take what you like and leave the rest." Well, I thought, I fought Him before, I'll just ignore Him now. I'll do it for her; after all, she took the time to bring me here and she's my friend.

I now have six years in Al-Anon. My friend stood by me and introduced me to a whole new way of life. God sent her to me, and she sent me to Al-Anon. Through the group, I became friends with God as I understand Him. He's loving, caring, compassionate and understanding. This is the recipe for a friend, and that He is.

Now, when I use the phrase, "Oh, my God," that's just what I mean. My God. It took me a long time to find Him. Al-Anon showed me where and how to find Him, and for that I say, "Thank God."

—*Anonymous*

I don't remember very much of my first few weeks in Al-Anon, but there was something there that I wanted to be part of. I was there because my fifteen-year-old son was in a center for alcohol dependency. The rehabilitation center strongly suggested that we should attend Al-Anon. After a few meetings, I became angry with those people around the table who seemed to be "fanatics" because they kept talking about God and spirituality. I had always been in contact with God. I went to religious classes and services every week. I knew words like, "faith," "belief," "sin" and—my favorites— "omnipotent" and "omnipresent." To me, they meant that you had to really watch it because God was always there watching, and if you were "bad," He had the power to punish and the ultimate power to banish you to hell. I was now sitting at the meetings, hearing people speak fondly of the Higher Power, while I was being "punished" (I had a son who was an alcoholic). So whenever they started talking about God, I would close my mind.

After about ten months in the program, I was discussing another "crisis" that had just occurred with my son, and my mother asked about it. I calmly remarked, "I wonder what positive thing God wants me to learn this time?" I was amazed that those words and that attitude were mine.

That evening, I spent hours thinking about God. I realized I had been given a great gift. I had always known a religion, but now I knew the spirituality that others talked about. I truly believed that God was a Loving Being. He wasn't keeping a scorecard. He wasn't punishing me.

He was giving me a chance to become a better person. No matter what twists and turns my life took, He was there and if I believed, I could find the good in any situation. If I truly believed that He was always there for me, I didn't have to worry or be fearful of things anymore.

For a year, I had been angry and resentful because I had had to give up my house, my friends, and all the things that were important to me because we moved to a new city. That night, I realized that the move had been part of a plan. A whole series of events had occurred that year that had led my son to find help in the rehabilitation center. I realized that all the things that had happened were not just coincidences; they were gifts from God. Thanks to Him, He also gave me the wisdom and courage to use these experiences positively. My son got help, and I got Al-Anon.

The Eleventh Step begins, "sought through prayer and meditation." I thought this was one Step I would never be able to take because, over the years, I had given up church and prayer. A few weeks ago, I was asked to speak on the

Eleventh Step. Since this Step had always eluded me, I didn't have any idea where to begin. I was handed a *Forum* article to read from. I realized as I read those words that I do listen. My whole life is God speaking to me. He tells me of love through my family and Al-Anon friends. He speaks of beauty in all the things around me: flowers, birds, mountains, grass, snow. He speaks to me of peace and serenity in laughter and time alone without being lonely. He quiets me by telling me of His unconditional love, and I know that I don't have to worry. He talks to me of acceptance. I accept the "good" in my life as His gift. I accept the "bad" as a gift given to help me learn such things as patience, unconditional love, or just how to be a better person. I have decided that if no other good can come from my son's disease, his pain will not have been worthless if I can be a better person with God's help and that of Al-Anon. I speak to God most often to help me accept others. We are all of His making. I may not like things others say or do, but they are all loved by Him and have a place in His plan.

Spirituality seemed so elusive because everything else in my life was tangible. This is something that just "is." Through the help of Al-Anon, I have realized that I am a person God can love. I have found Him within myself. He is a part of me. He is omnipotent: if I listen, He guides me. He is omnipresent: He is always with me. I have gained the elusive "happiness" I never seemed able to find. All I had to do was accept it. I was always searching for that thing or person who would give it to me, when all along He had given it to me and it was within me. With His guidance, I am now responsible for my life.

I thank God for showing me the way to Al-Anon so that I could find Him.

—*Anonymous*

For much of my life, words like "God" and "spiritual" meant only one thing to me: organized religion. I was reared as a member of a large, Protestant denomination and had normal involvement within the congregation as a child and teenager. Instead of feeling a sense of love and comfort in this environment, I felt a sense of being different and apart. I can remember coming home from church and feeling I was going to hell because I was a bad person. How bad can you be at eleven years of age?

Later in life, as a result of loving alcoholics, my life became a battleground in which I vacillated between a blind, hopeless faith in God and anger at Him over the reality of my situation.

Al-Anon gave me courage by giving me first-hand knowledge of how others had changed themselves and their circumstances. I saw glimpses of serenity as I realized I was beginning to think more clearly; I understood wisdom when I made some small decision and it worked out well. I still did not see God, but I saw a lot of people who gave me love and hope with every meeting and every phone call.

After a while, I began to understand words and phrases that helped make sense of my spiritual struggle. When I heard "conscious contact," I knew I did not know how to make that contact. God was still abstract to me. I guess I expected a knock on the door or a knock on the head to indicate a spiritual awakening. But the knocks never came. Instead, I experienced an "occasional awareness" of a changed attitude or a changed behavior. It was recognition of my changed behavior that convinced me that a spiritual being of some force was at work in my life. I was waking up to God, a God of love and acceptance. He is a God who allows me to find Him in everyone I meet. This God is a God of comfort and peace, a God for everyday use. He is a God of my awareness who serves as a guide in all areas of my life.

Today, I know that my Creator only wants what is best for me. As long as I am open to His will for me, I know that He will grant me courage, serenity and wisdom. My God is visible, for He is at work in the lives of Al-Anon members throughout the world.

—*Pennsylvania, United States*

93

I had trouble with Step Two because the only Power I knew was the God I grew up with and I wanted no part of Him. So I made up a prayer: "If there really is a power out there, or anywhere, who cares about me, let me know. The mailbox is open; send a letter."

I'd say or think this appeal on my drive to work each morning. After a week or two, I got my letter. I had a dream in which I was going to meet my Higher Power. I climbed up a staircase in a house, not knowing what to expect, and opened a door. Inside was a room with a big, comfortable bed. It was spread with a patchwork quilt and propped against the pillow was my very own Higher Power. She looked like a kindly grandmother as she patted a place on the bed to invite me to sit down and talk to her.

When I awoke, the visualization of my Higher Power and the deep feeling of peace stayed with me. As a result, I was able to completely change my concept of God. My Higher Power has worked within me and today I recognize her with many faces, but only one personality; She is always loving and always available.

To recover in Al-Anon, I don't have to call my Higher Power "God." I don't have to pray any certain prayer, just as I don't have to have blond hair or white skin or money in the bank.

—*Arizona, United States*

The Al-Anon program has not changed my religion, but it has enhanced my spirituality and my relationship with God.

I was brought up in a very religious home and regularly attended Sunday School and church services. But the God they acquainted me with was in heaven, a God to be worshipped and revered but beyond my reach for any closer relationship.

During the many long years of drinking I tried to pray, but I was frustrated by this apparent distance between us. I was never sure that my prayers were reaching Him, especially when I didn't seem to be getting any answers.

Now, the Twelve Steps of our beautiful Al-Anon program have given me a completely new concept of God. His presence is with me constantly, and I can talk with Him as a friend. There are no more formal prayers, but instead conversation with someone who understands and cares for me.

Since I have been a widow, I have been faced with many decisions, and I have learned to rely on my God. I have talked with Him about my problems, weighing the pros and cons and asking His guidance. Then, after much deliberation and careful thought, I can arrive at a decision confident that it is the right one. I have received "the power to carry that out." God is working in my life, but we must be a team. He cannot do it alone.

I'm so grateful to the Al-Anon program for enhancing my spirituality and altering my relationship with the God of my childhood.

—*Iowa, United States*

One thing that made me nearly miss the Al-Anon program was my spiritual pride. I thought that these things they taught were things I had known all my life, and the only reason I kept going back was because my husband's sponsor pointed out to me that those people were happy and I was not. Possibly, they had something to impart.

So when I heard them talking so much about the grace of God, I listened, even though I felt sure I knew the meaning of the term. And sure enough, I knew the dictionary definition: "the unmerited favor of God, the undeserved goodness of God." And I remembered someone who once told me: "You can't always go by a dictionary. The dictionary says that a dog is a four-legged canine animal, but if you've ever had one, you know that's not a complete definition." Well, I've had a few dogs, so I knew that was right.

I believe that God's grace also means that God is doing for us what we cannot do for ourselves.

He floods my life with His grace, doing things for me and through me that I could never do myself. He uses me in the lives of other people, and He sees that there is time for everything I need to do. When I try running things myself, they end up in a mess. So I surrender.

—*Texas, United States*

Before Al-Anon, I remember standing at my kitchen window, full of melancholy, wondering where my laughter had gone. If I did laugh, it was hollow and infrequent.

When I first heard laughter in the program, I wondered how we could make light of the pain and heartache. But laughter heals, and I have accepted that it is a way to come to terms with those feelings we have buried and can hardly face. Now I look for the humor in every situation, and my Higher Power is a laughing God who reminds me not to take myself too seriously.

—*New York, United States*

When I heard in Al-Anon that God is everything and I heard the idea discussed at meetings, I was puzzled. Then one day, I was driving home from a meeting and I saw a strong and handsome young man in a sleek red convertible. Suddenly, it hit me. God is strength. God is power. God is virility. Those attributes are from God, no matter how one may use them. I realized how negative my interpretations had been. I saw trees in bloom. God is sunshine, light. God is laughter, God is growth. I saw a young couple holding hands; God is love and intimacy. God is . . . a chair? Yes, for God is support. Everything I saw could be translated into the abstract quality that further defined God as I understand Him/Her.

--Texas, United States

After a short time in Al-Anon, I had been praying for closeness to my Higher Power. While relating this at an Al-Anon meeting, I realized that I had this closeness and didn't feel separated from God any more, even though I did not know when this had taken place.

Since that time, there have been events that strengthened my faith. One was that our 18-year-old daughter was dating someone we did not like. We did all the wrong things and made all the mistakes parents make. It looked as if they were going to marry despite our objections. As always, my style was to mess up as long as I could, until I could do nothing at all, and then I turned it over to God. I admitted I was powerless over this situation and asked for guidance. Several events led me to prayer, and I realized that God loved my child more than I did and would take care of her if I would only get out of the way. So I released her with love. I realized I did not know what was best for my child, myself, or anyone else. I became willing to stand by and watch her go through whatever it took for her to find her peace with a God of her understanding.

Al-Anon has shown me how to grow spiritually, to shake loose from the dogma and rigidity of the religion that I had been indoctrinated in, and find the freedom to know God personally. I don't need to go through any creed, formal litany, or particular mediator. I have a one-to-one personal contact with the God of my understanding. I think of Him as my Creator, my Savior, my Provider, and my Friend. I equate His love to that of a true parent's love, though many times greater.

Parents love each of their children equally, know their potential and capabilities individually, assign tasks and expect results accordingly. As a slow child improves or progresses, the parents assign more and more difficult tasks. They expect more as the child's capabilities grow, but they do not love less if there is inadequacy. The parents may be sad or disappointed, even hurt, because one child doesn't fulfill its potential, but their love remains the same. The parents encourage growth but never punish for lack of it. They rejoice at each accomplishment and sometimes cry at failures because of the pain the child experiences, but they never withdraw their love, support or help. They stand by and watch the turmoil in the child with a heavy heart until the child reaches out to them. The parents' love is steadfast and true. They know it is human nature to change only when the pain grows unbearable. To stop the pain would stop the progress. They wait for surrender, then take the child in their arms and kiss away the pain and lead the child through the crisis. Through each struggle, the child becomes stronger and better prepared to handle the next hurdle of life.

In Al-Anon, I have experienced God in this way and I have found Him always there, waiting, willing and able, but I have to surrender each problem to Him and ask for His help.

—*Alabama, United States*

God as I understand Him knows what I need without my mentioning my needs to Him. He knows what I want and what I'm thinking at the same time I do, and He is able to sort out the important things from the ramblings or awkward wording when I talk to Him, in the same way that my very dear friends do for me. He knows that I don't always know what's going on inside me or why I feel so scared at times, and He is able to send His messengers ahead of the situation to make the way clear. He usually waits until I ask for help, but He knows my heart. Even before my lips ask Him, He hears the urgency of my heart and begins to send reinforcements.

— *Texas, United States*

Early one morning, while there was a hushed stillness on the land and each tree stood motionless, I looked up at the sky. There, bands of white clouds hung suspended. The different textures of the streaks caught my interest. Some were smooth; others were ripples like sand on a beach. As I watched them, I suddenly realized that the entire mass was in motion. An unseen force was driving them eastward. That force was a wind invisible to my eye, and yet it had such power. All I could see of it was the effects of its power.

My life, too, has something propelling it, even though I don't feel any motion where I stand. Too often, I remain unaware of it because I cannot see, touch, taste or smell it. Yet I can make contact with that Power greater than myself. And when I recognize it, I feel less buffeted and tossed about. There is also gentleness in that force; when I learn to move with it, it cradles and protects me.

The spiritual awakening that came to me through the Al-Anon Steps shows me how to find and use that unseen force in every area of my life, One Day at a Time.

—*New York, United States*

My Higher Power is a combination of a whole lot of things that have become part of me and the strength I now have. It is, perhaps, a state of mind. It is the awareness of many incidents that have taken place over which I had no control, when other people or circumstances played a major role in my life, without my awareness.

My Higher Power was in those members who, when I first came to Al-Anon, assured me that I would get help and gave me the incentive to come out of my shell and be less afraid. They gave me the courage to try, and the fear gradually left because I did succeed in some things.

Or, in the case of failure, there were those around me who would tell me that it was not the end of the world, that this, too, would pass. And now my Higher Power is the confidence within me that makes me unafraid, even unafraid to make mistakes.

My Higher Power is the joy that is sometimes within me when I know that I am glad to be alive and can appreciate what is beautiful. It is that sense of peace that comes to me when I take time to have a quiet time and relax and be at peace with the world.

Or is it that intangible force that helps me say the right thing when someone in need cries out for help and I feel inadequate on my own to give that help?

My Higher Power is the unexpected telephone call when I am feeling blue or full of self-pity, or the sun coming out to brighten the day, or that line in some piece of literature that springs up from the page and is just what I need to help me over a sticky patch. I am not religious, but that does not matter. This is a spiritual, not a religious program. I still don't understand: it is often "God as I *don't* understand Him."

But I have a Higher Power, and my spirit that was dead is now alive, active and unafraid. It works.

—*Anonymous*

Springtime is an uplifting season. It is so much like Al-Anon, so full of rebirth and new growth. Preparing the garden soil and planting the seeds, I see as my responsibility. But the miracle of seeds sprouting and growing into productive plants lies with a Power beyond human power.

In Al-Anon, I have to take responsibility for going to meetings, reading literature and practicing the program to the best of my ability. But the miracle of my growth I attribute to my Higher Power. When I am willing to change, it is this Power that causes the change. Sometimes the growth is so gradual I have to look back in retrospect to see its real extent.

I have to recognize the faults I want to be rid of, just as I must be able to recognize the weeds that need to be pulled from my garden.

Pruning is like discipline. I don't like to prune established plants or thin those that are becoming overcrowded, yet for their own healthy development, this must be done. I'm not good at discipline either, but for my own good, I must have a measure of self-discipline.

I think of the bedding plants I set out in my garden and how I protect them with some temporary shelter from the hot sun and wind until they have become rooted and strong enough to withstand the elements. That reminds me of how I sometimes need shelter against the elements of living, but I cannot lean indefinitely on the support of the group or my sponsor, even though such support is ever-present. My goal in Al-Anon is not to be sheltered from all adversity, but to become rooted securely in that Power that will sustain me through all problems.

—*Manitoba, Canada*

Traveling to the sites of ancient civilizations, seeing the beauty of their monuments, is a humbling experience. I've just returned from a trip through Greece, the islands of the Aegean and parts of Asia Minor. I had one overwhelming impression from these places of antiquity. What remains is their memorials to whatever each worshipped as the Power greater than themselves: the sacred horns and labyrinth of the palace at Crete, the grave of Agamemnon at Mycenae, the temple of Zeus at Olympia.

The search for a Higher Power, plus the need for release from the ravages of alcoholism, dates way back. In sun-drenched Greece, Apollo, the sun god, was an important deity and they also paid tribute to Dionysus, the god of wine. Seeing Ephesus and Corinth, which figure so largely in early Christian writings, was unforgettable. It was stirring to realize these were the paths the apostle Paul took before he wrote his letters to the Ephesians, telling them, "Be not drunk with wine, wherein is excess, but be filled with the spirit."

Similarly, the modern attractions of a country include those dedicated to a belief in God: mosques and minarets in Istanbul, picturesque whitewashed churches perched above the harbors of Greek islands. Also, the bond with people of other nations is often their beliefs. On a quiet fishing island, I talked with a charming old gentleman, he in halting English and I in pidgin Greek. We had the common link of each having a daughter in the state of Vermont, and he told me how much it meant to him to have dinner in a small Vermont town last year with the local banker and mayor and to see that they, too, said a prayer before meals.

I appreciate the broad-mindedness of our fellowship, wherein each one of us is free to worship the God of our understanding. How grateful I am to Al-Anon for the spiritual awakening that led me to believe in a Power beyond myself. Now, I can sense the spiritual connection between different peoples and feel the force of a Higher Power in diverse settings. Yet, I don't need to be in a sacred spot to be in touch with the God of my understanding. I can make contact each time I listen with an open heart, or reach out in love.

I sensed one more lesson as I saw the imposing stone ruins of ancient times: though life is to be lived one day at a time, there is a continuity of existence. Knowing that our roots go back a long way gives us stability, and realizing that the end of everything is not here and now gives us hope.

—*New York, United States*

4

Recognizing Spiritual Awakenings

Step Twelve states that we will have "a spiritual awakening as the result of these Steps." It doesn't say when or where we will have that experience or what it will be. The nature of the experience varies with the individual. But the experience of Al-Anon members suggests that when it happens, we will know intuitively and a new level of perception will open up to us. We feel there will be no doubt in our minds because a Power greater than ourselves can communicate a presence in our lives uniquely, according to our needs.

In this chapter, several Al-Anon members share their spiritual awakenings. They range from the subtle to the dramatic. A member from Kentucky writes: "I had heard of a spiritual awakening I was supposed to have in Al-Anon. I kept waiting for a big bolt of lightning or something equally dramatic. But I've never had a spiritual experience, as such. It just sort of crept up on me. For the first time in my life, I do not worry. I know God is with me always. I feel His presence every minute of the day. I know that whatever happens in my life, I will be okay." Other members have had sudden experiences of understanding the larger concerns of the universe, giving them a temporary reprieve from focusing on the human condition. Still others have felt their oneness with nature and defined this as a spiritual awakening.

For all who have had spiritual awakenings, life

takes on a different quality; their lives will never again be the same. Most people find it very difficult to articulate these experiences. A member from South Carolina tells of relating such an occurrence. She had told a spiritual adviser that she had "intense feelings of rebirth" as a result of working the Twelve Steps. She felt "bright-eyed, eager to experience new things," trusting, happy, and filled with self-acceptance. He shared her joy and said, "Personally, I don't care how and where it happens, just so long as it does."

If we follow the Twelve Steps to the best of our abilities, we will be led to a new life, one that far surpasses our wildest imaginings and most earnest yearnings before Al-Anon. As one member from New York stated, "A deeper understanding of what it means to be human leads inevitably toward a source of wisdom and power outside the self."

The first time I ever heard the Twelve Steps read at a meeting, I became very still. I felt I was not breathing, that time and space had become irrelevant, and I was just listening with my whole being. I became aware of a force around my shoulders, holding me motionless in my chair. It seemed as if I could reach up and touch it, but I was so compelled by what I was hearing that I just let it be. It was more important to me to hear the words than to confirm what was to me a palpable presence. Whatever it was, it helped me concentrate on every word that was being said. And when the words were finished, I knew deep within me that I was "home." I understood intuitively the meaning of "grace." I knew that I had received the gift of hope, the chance to live life well and in the presence of good people. I knew that a direction was being offered to me which was not yet clear, but which was clearly desirable. I left that meeting in a state of elation, knowing without doubt that I would return.

—*Wisconsin. United States*

One of the most difficult tasks for me in Al-Anon was to find a God of my understanding. No matter how hard I tried, I stumbled along in darkness and in fear. Then, I heard an AA member say that every morning he put his will and his life into God's care. To me, that was like the sunrise, and I sat overwhelmed by the beauty and simplicity of it! I have walked in the daylight ever since. Although there have been dark clouds and some frightening thunderstorms, there has never again been complete darkness, and some days the sunshine brings out all the bright colors and puts a smile on all the faces I see. I have found a power greater than fear. I have found the God of my understanding.

—*Australia*

On Thanksgiving several years ago, I was newly divorced and feeling lonely. I'd been dating a woman and was driving to her home, full of self-pity for not being with "my" family and fearful of how I would behave with her relatives, and suddenly I felt alone. Just as suddenly a warm feeling engulfed my body when I realized, "Hey, I'm not alone. I've got all those warm friends in Al-Anon who love me and I'm going to see them at the meeting tonight. Even if I don't do or say the right things at dinner, I will be loved anyway." I started to laugh, sing and cry and was full of a deep sense of gratitude for what I did have. I had a great time at dinner. That night at the meeting, I wept when I shared my experience and had that same overwhelming feeling of gratitude.

—*Connecticut, United States*

The faraway honkings of a flock of geese caused me to halt in my rush and look up. For some reason, I noticed one particular goose on that cold autumn day. My head was still reeling from my day's work, and my heart was heavy with dread knowing that I would be faced with the problems of my husband's alcoholism when I arrived at home. Day after day, his illness imposed itself on our household, but in spite of that, life had to go on.

I stood there for a long time. I looked up and allowed myself to think about that one goose in the middle of the flock. She was working very hard, flying against the wind. I thought she must be just as tired as I, and the cold wind ruffled her feathers. Now and then, she would honk, yet she persevered. What inner voice guided her to labor so? What Higher Power set her in the world to travel on her course? "Look!" we say, "there go the geese. Winter must be coming." What about the exhausted goose? She does her job. She builds her nest. She lays her eggs. She raises her young. Every day she finds food for herself. And every year at the proper season, she must lift her wings to leave it all and begin again with nothing but the tail feathers of the next goose to guide her. Yet, we notice her comings and goings and know that she belongs. To us, she and her flock are a marvel to mark our changing seasons, and we give them an appreciation they can't understand.

"And what about me?" I asked. "I do my job, tend my house, and labor under difficulties, too.

Could it be that God knows the purpose, if I do not? Do I have a place in the order of the universe even though I may not at the moment comprehend it?"

At last, the flock out of sight, I continued on my way home. But my strength was renewed, and my heart was no longer heavy. Gratitude had lifted my spirits, and I gave thanks for that wonderful moment of peace.

—*Manitoba, Canada*

As we were winding our way down the path, coming back from the beach, we could hear how still the woods had become, with only the sound of what seemed like soft, gentle rain. But looking up, we saw it wasn't rain at all. Many spruce needles were falling like rain onto the trees and bushes. For a moment, I became very still and very aware of the beautiful tall, strong trees that had endured all kinds of weather through the years. As I looked down, I could see many shades of green, and I was reminded of a rain forest. I could hear a stream in the background, and birds were singing. It was truly beautiful!

For another moment, I was totally caught up by the presence of my Higher Power and how powerful and strong He is to me. I felt no fear. I felt safe and protected, as free as the birds. A few tears of joy came to my eyes.

—*Oregon, United States*

Since boyhood, I have spent many vacations at the Jersey shore. I have strolled miles of its beaches and boardwalks, sunbathed on its soft sands, swam and fished in its incessant surf, and sailed its length from Sandy Hook to Cape May.

I have seen and heard the Atlantic rage during a hurricane, thundering over bulkheads and breakwaters. I have watched as a house was crushed in minutes by its power. I have seen ocean-front homes that had been lifted intact, as if made of origami, onto the grassy banks of the distant inland lagoons.

Like persons who live facing the Atlantic, we

in Al-Anon come to recognize our dependence on a Power greater than ourselves. We gain increasing respect for what it can do. We commit less and less of our energy in futile efforts to control persons and situations around us, and more and more in harnessing its enormous creative strength to gain control over our own lives.

As an Alateen member once put it, her decision to turn her will and life over to the care of God came only after she had come to experience "the feel of cactus and the taste of tears" in her daily life.

Yet, it also takes faith that a Power greater than ourselves, working through the program, can convert our desperation into an ongoing healing experience.

Later, as we begin to obtain the rewards of spiritual growth, despite setbacks, we come to regard the tasks of daily living less as burdens and more as opportunities. In our new wisdom, we come to accept our limited role in the alcoholic situation. We are closer to a life course that puts the wind behind our sails.

During my boyhood vacations at the shore, I recall lying in bed at night, listening to the familiar beat of the surf. I am still possessed by this sound. These heartbeats of creation help me to align myself with the rhythm of nature. Once again, I become acutely aware of the wholeness of the world, the renewing power of life.

—*New Jersey, United States*

For the first year and a half in Al-Anon, I was hanging on by a thread. Gone were my self-esteem and self-confidence. In a short span of time, my marriage and career were gone, followed closely by the final blow, bankruptcy. Everything I had worked for was gone. In order to maintain my sanity, I filled my days with Al-Anon meetings.

After some time, I developed a need to return to my home town and my parents' gravesite. Many years had passed since I had stood at that place. The day was filled with the beauty of

121

spring. Standing on that spot, I was suddenly filled with sadness and shame. I talked to my parents with tears in my eyes. I asked if they were proud of me. The answer came back as if spoken from above: Yes, they were.

This was the most moving experience of my life. My parents would have trusted that I would do the best I could under the circumstances. I realized that I was a good, loving, worthwhile person.

—*Wisconsin, United States*

After six years in Al-Anon, I was asked to share my story at an AA convention. I agreed to do so, with apprehension, fear and anticipation. I knew this would be a giant step in growth for me, so I immediately put the Eleventh Step to work. God and I had several conversations!

I asked family members and some Al-Anon members for prayerful support in this endeavor. The day finally arrived. I started out by asking God to take charge of my day and asked that His will be done. Much to my surprise and delight, one of my brothers and his wife came to hear me.

I started my story: "To the best of my knowledge, alcoholism was not a problem in my growing-up years." I went on to mention that my father was violent, my mother was a hypochondriac, and the word "love" was never mentioned in our home. I continued talking about my life as I understood it. When I finished, I silently thanked God and gave Him all the compliments I received.

The next day, I visited my brother. He asked me why I had said that alcoholism was not a problem in my childhood. "Don't you remember the liquor hidden in the furnace? Or how our parents would come in drunk and fighting?" I was flabbergasted! Yes, I did remember! The more we talked, the more God revealed to me and the more astonished I became. I couldn't believe that, with all the time I had spent in Al-Anon and the things I had learned about alcoholism, I had never realized I was also the child of alcoholic parents.

I drove home with mixed emotions— awe, gratitude and disbelief. I had come to believe that God was in charge of me, that He has my whole life planned and will make me aware of things in His own time.

—*Florida, United States*

In the years before Al-Anon, I was consumed with my sorry lot in life. I knew there was a God out there somewhere, but I didn't really feel He was part of my life. When I asked Him to make my husband stop drinking or to make my children conform to my wishes for them, my desires were not met, so I doubted that God even knew I existed. I took my body to church, but my mind and soul stayed home and receded into an invisible cocoon, where I was shutting myself up with despair and self-pity. I felt that no one understood, not even God.

My children were almost grown, and the knowledge that in a few more years I would no longer be responsible for them kept me going.

That was the only light at the end of the tunnel that I could see. Then, I thought, I could leave all this, and my life would be better.

Then the crisis came, and I really hit bottom. At the age of forty-two, I found I was pregnant again. What made this news even more bitter was that it came a year after my husband's vasectomy. How could God allow such a thing to happen! Didn't He know that I already had all the misery I could stand?

About this time, I began reaching out for help to my pastor, my doctor, and marriage counselor. And each of them tried to guide me to Al-Anon. So I went a few times, but how indignant I was at first! I was trying to find out how I could change the persons in my life who were causing me pain, but these people were telling me that I couldn't change other people, that I should work on changing myself and my attitude. What gall they had! I didn't feel it was I who needed changing.

But not knowing where else to turn, I kept going to Al-Anon. Slowly, I began to open my mind and ears to what was being said. "Let Go and Let God," they said. "Pray only for knowledge of His will and the power to carry that out."

My doctor, who had seen my complete collapse into despair over the pregnancy, offered to arrange an abortion for me. As I had always had strong feelings against abortion, I felt much ambivalence over this. If I had ever needed someone to tell me what to do, I needed that now! But who? And more strongly than I had ever felt anything before, I began to get the message—not in any great flash of lightning or anything of that sort, but just by praying, "Please God, help me! Show me what you want me to do."

Well, I had this beautiful baby girl, and I've loved her with all my heart from the moment she was born! She's ten years old now and she's given me the incentive to change myself and ultimately, my life. God knew I needed her, and I firmly believe it was He who helped me come to know that I did.

From the moment that crisis brought me to my

knees and I began to trust that God would lead me through each day if I let Him, many changes began to take place. I started looking for the good in every situation, and gradually my self-pity left me. In this past ten years, four members of my family have stopped drinking or using drugs, and together we are all recovering from the family disease.

—*Minnesota, United States*

Although my husband had been sober for a year, there was still unpleasantness at home, and a good AA friend urged me to join Al-Anon.

The group was brand new and all of us were newcomers, so we began at the beginning and went through the Twelve Steps. The first eleven didn't seem to apply to me. "Powerless over alcohol?" It was my husband who had the drinking problem. "Remove my shortcomings?" I was the one who was holding everything together. I decided to ignore the preliminaries and jumped immediately to the middle part of the Twelfth

Step—carrying the message to others. Needless to say, problems continued at home.

One day, several years later, as I walked toward a busy intersection with an Al-Anon friend, I continued in my usual fashion about my husband and his lack of improvement. Unexpectedly, my friend grabbed me by the shoulders and shook me.

"I'm tired of hearing your whining complaints," she said. "It's time you really began working on you. Begin with the First Step."

I was so stunned by her reaction that I listened. After we both calmed down, we discussed the First Step and the meaning of powerlessness. It made good sense; why hadn't I heard it before? A curious sense of relief came over me. I sensed I was still making my life miserable because I couldn't release the controls.

As I look back at this incident today, I realize it was the beginning of a spiritual awakening that made me ready to go back over the Steps and apply them with greater care to my life. I stopped speaking for a while and didn't hop over to new-comers to fill their ears with empty words. Instead, I made a conscious effort to listen to the message others so willingly shared with me.

Slowly, I began to search for my Higher Power and, at the same time, became ready and willing to see my shortcomings and faults. I had been asking others to teach me serenity, but it was there all the time if only I had not ignored the Steps. Miraculously, for the first time in my life, I sensed the presence of a spiritual force outside myself. I felt humbled by my new awareness, and love gradually replaced the bitterness within me. I was aware that a dramatic change had taken place. A new set of values, a new and exciting life are mine. I believe this was a spiritual awakening.

Practicing the principles of the Al-Anon program has to be a daily effort for me if I am to keep the spirit within me awake and alert. Then, and only then, have I the right to carry the message to others.

—*Connecticut, United States*

Serenity is like gravity; you can't see it and you can't touch it, but you can feel it.
—*Virginia, United States*

I came into Al-Anon an agnostic and a firm believer in free will. I was given a brain and I believed it should be used to think for myself, that I should stand on my own two feet, make my own decisions and not let any setback overwhelm me. I was a very dominant, independent, determined individual. But I was very tired of being the strong one and carrying all the worries, fears and troubles around on my shoulders. I finally decided to give this Higher Power a chance.

I decided to try "Let Go and Let God" on one tiny little thing. Amazingly, it worked! Then I tried it on a few other little things, gradually working up to bigger problems and they also turned out well.

I came to believe in a personal Higher Power and at the same time, I made the decision to turn my life and will over to God. By striving to remove my shortcomings and changing my attitudes, I became a spiritual being. If I remain constant in my attitude of faith and courage, outer changes do not make me fearful and do not disturb me because I know God is at work in and through me in all the affairs of my life. As I change and grow spiritually, I attain an inner stability, become more poised and serene, confident and fearless. Truth is changeless and its spirit enables me to be flexible, resilient, open and teachable. Love and forgiveness, joy and understanding are changeless. This understanding enables me to live happily in the world, undismayed by outer changes. I have faith that all things are working together for good.

—*Ohio, United States*

Many concepts and phrases aren't really heard by us until we are ready to hear them in our hearts. I remember the first time that I heard, "Let Go and Let God." I had no comprehension of what it meant, but I was startled because I didn't understand it. It was amazing to me that I had never heard it before. Everyone else seemed to understand it perfectly. So I meditated on the concept and I began to feel its impact on my life immediately. I didn't need to carry unnecessary burdens anymore. God was there to handle the burdens that I could not.

This was only a small awakening, and I have had many since then, some more dramatic than others, but when one of these clear moments comes, I am always left with a feeling that the truth which has been revealed to me is so obvious that I wonder how I could have missed it for so long. And experience has taught me, too, that these truths have a way of fading and that sometimes, I need rude reminders of them if I begin to neglect my spiritual program. But they always remain close to my consciousness and I know that the way I perceive the world has been permanently changed as a result of the Al-Anon program.

—*Indiana, United States*

Like so many others, I arrived at the door of my first Al-Anon meeting, more than twenty years ago, spiritually and emotionally bereft. My husband's alcoholism and his newfound sobriety in AA overshadowed my entire being. The slightest hint that he might again pick up a drink left me in a total state of panic and dread.

With the passage of time and faithful attendance at weekly Al-Anon meetings, the emotional aspect of my problem began to improve, although it took many years of Al-Anon to find a firmer footing.

The spiritual side of my life was in shambles. As a child, I had balked at the idea of receiving any formal religious training, and my parents did not force the issue. In my adult years, out of a sense of guilt and perhaps fear, I made a few feeble starts at finding God, but I never followed through. To justify these failures, I assured myself that God was only a myth, created by and for weak people who could not stand on their own feet. Hence, if I needed a God to rely on, it must be concluded that I was also weak. Then I created a second myth to convince myself that I was exceedingly strong and that godlike, I could endure just about anything and control everything, including my husband's drinking problem.

Needless to say, I was in a lot of trouble, particularly since the Al-Anon philosophy could not co-exist with my own omnipotence. Something had to change; quite reluctantly, I admitted that it had to be me. Giving just an inch, but not a fraction more, I promised myself that I would again search for this Higher Power my group talked about all the time. Then the idea came, "Why not use the group as this Higher Power?" For a time, this seemed to work. But then arrived the day when disagreements within the group caused uncertainties and my new-found Higher Power revealed its clay feet. "What now?" I asked.

The answer evolved, as it usually does, in the guise of a personal crisis. I was suddenly faced

with the possibility of losing custody of my two
sons to my former husband, who re-entered our
lives after an absence of many years. I was terrified. My Al-Anon friends urged me to turn to
prayer. But who was I to pray to? With no other
choice in the midst of this madness, I felt I had
nothing to lose by trying to turn to this God, a
God I did not understand. At first, I tested God
by saying, "If you're really the God you're supposed to be, see to it that I retain custody of my
boys. Please!" But the reply I sensed wasn't
what I wanted nor expected. "Why not seek
acceptance of My will instead?" What a humbling experience! I detested it. But it was the
turning point in my life and, in a sense, it prepared me for the greatest challenge of my life-
time which I was to face six years later.

Though I had maintained custody of my sons
after all, my younger son, at the age of twelve,
asked to spend time with his father, who lived in
another state. Through Al-Anon, I had gained
greater confidence in myself as a mother, so I
agreed that he could spend his summer vacation

at his father's home, but extracted a promise at the same time that he would return in time for school in the fall. This, however, was a promise he would not be able to keep. The boy I had fought so hard for lost his life in a bicycling accident on unfamiliar roads.

Through the clouds of grief, despair and shock, my one recurring thought was, "How can I ever accept this?" Never had the reality of powerlessness been more evident. I had not been given any choices.

Despite my unwillingness to accept the fact that my child had been cut down so young, I knew that I could never again allow blame, fear and other negative aspects of my pre-Al-Anon existence to overpower me. In a moment of insight, I had reached another crossroads in my relationship to a Higher Power. I could deny Him once again—or I could reach out and reaffirm my faith and trust.

After several weeks of wrestling, I came to see that my son's life would have been lived in vain if I reverted to the person I had once been—shallow, demanding, egocentric. In this I did have a choice. I chose to move forward, toward my Higher Power, whom I now acknowledge as God, in the realization that I have been given a special precious gift, a belief in a power greater than myself.

—*Connecticut, United States*

After months of planning and preparation, we were finally on our way to take a vacation—something we had not done since our children were young, twenty years before. With my husband's encouragement and my family's enthusiastic support, I had terminated my employment and had completed the requirements to continue my education. We were going on our motorcycle, which I really enjoyed. I would never have done it until the days of sobriety. This was going to be a truly special two-week holiday, and I firmly believed that God of my understanding helps those who help themselves!

In early evening on the second day, seven hundred miles from home, in a nearby but unfamiliar state, we made our last stop before traveling to the isolated area that was our destination for the night. As we rested on a picnic bench in the cool shade of a tree, I saw a coin at my feet. When I picked it up, "In God We Trust" was what I first saw. My husband told me to put it in my pocket as a reminder of that thought.

We resumed our trip and soon came to a construction zone with a sign warning of loose gravel. Suddenly, we lost control of the bike and were propelled into the air. I remember the fleeting thought that I was alive, just before I landed with a thud. My next awareness was of my husband lying motionless and bleeding some distance from me, but when I tried to get to him, I couldn't move. Totally immobilized, lying in the gravel, I could no longer help myself.

Soon a concerned and competent young man stopped and went into action. A minute later, another vehicle arrived, and the driver offered assistance. In a very short time, people seemed to be coming from nowhere, offering whatever they had for our comfort. In some instances, the offerings were material, but one young lady offered her unceasing physical touch and soft voice for forty-five minutes until the ambulance arrived. I believe that the God of my understanding was presenting Himself to me through her.

Always the eternal optimist, it never occurred to me that this could be more than an inconvenient delay in our holiday. The emergency team at the hospital scrubbed the gravel out of our bodies, X-rayed us, poked and probed and stitched, and assured us that we were very lucky. Nurses carefully bathed me and then gently lifted me into bed onto soft pillows and ice bags. The God of my understanding was making His presence known to me through these kind, gentle people who were taking care of me.

As the initial physical shock started to lessen and the pain began to intensify, the findings of our conditions were presented to us. In addition to the abrasions and bruises, we both had broken bones. My husband had suffered four broken ribs. My left ankle and right foot were both fractured. No problem, I thought, because I have always enjoyed doing things with my hands, but never had enough time to do them. Then I was told that I had five impacted joint fractures in my right hand. So I reassured myself that at least I could still talk, even though I was finding it increasingly difficult and painful to move my mouth, and a large bruise was beginning to appear on my jaw.

A couple we had met in the program came to drive us back home. They made the trip a comfortable one, and I had no choice but to ask my Al-Anon sister for help with even my most basic needs. After we got home, my husband and family also assisted me, and the God of my understanding revealed Himself to me through all those caring people.

Then my doctor discovered I had a fractured jaw that needed to be wired shut. Only one activity was now available to me: meditation. I was given many long and painful weeks to meditate. And now I understand with a new awareness certain events in my life's journey. I began to realize that my God had been appearing to me in human beings that I had been forced to ask for help. Only then did I know that I could ask Him for help directly. So when I prayed to Him for help to bear the unendurable pain in my jaw, He allowed me to physically feel the release of tension in each individual muscle of my body, starting at the top of my head and ending at the tips of my toes.

—*Wyoming, United States*

God doesn't always cure us, but He can always heal us.

—*New York, United States*

If my problems have brought me to prayer, then they have served a purpose.

—*Maryland, United States*

Sometimes it is reassuring to see a "sign" that tells me I am making the right decision. Some people would call these signs coincidences, but I choose to see them as affirmations.

I had come to the painful decision that it would be best for me to move away from the small town I had been living in for three years. I had friends, but the funding for my job was uncertain, and the town was so small that there were few opportunities to pursue. I decided to move to a large city 500 miles away. Packed and ready to leave my apartment, I walked through it one last time to make sure I had everything I wanted. I noticed a plant hanging by the window. It belonged to me, but it looked so beautiful in that spot that I couldn't bear to take it down. I wrestled with the decision to leave it because the container had been made by workers in a sheltered workshop for mentally retarded adults. I had known several of the workers and I knew that the plant hanger would be a reminder of them and their affection for me. Yet I also knew that the people who were renting the apartment would enjoy the plant in its present location. So I turned away and left the plant in the apartment.

I had one last visit to make on my way out of town. A couple who had been very supportive of me through a troubled time lived just a few miles away, and I felt the need to say good-bye to them. So I stopped and chatted and told them how helpful they had been to me. As I was getting ready to leave, and they were walking me to my car, the man, who worked at the sheltered workshop, said, "Just a minute—I've been meaning to give you something." And he walked out to his garage and brought back not one but three plant hangers like the one I had just left!

--*Ohio, United States*

When I came into Al-Anon, God wasn't in the picture. I wasn't for Him or against Him, I just wasn't with Him. I sat in the meetings and listened to everyone else talk about a Higher Power, God as they understood Him. They never tried to make me believe in anything. In fact, the closest anyone came to imposing an idea on me was when they said, "You don't have to believe in anything; you just believe that I believe."

This wasn't a hard request, for I could see the smiles on their faces and the sparkle in their eyes. When my sponsor talked, there was a glow all around her. She seemed to have a halo over her head. I remember batting my eyes because I wasn't sure of what I was seeing. These people talked a lot about hope and faith. They had it; I wanted it.

In the older edition of *Living With an Alcoholic* (now retitled, *Al-Anon Family Groups*) under Step Two, it says that "some may not have what is sometimes called the 'gift of faith.' " That was me. I didn't have faith in anything that I couldn't hear, see or touch. I suppose that is why I used the group and my sponsor as my Higher Power in the beginning.

After a short time in the program, however, some strange things started happening. I will share one of them with you.

We were very poor. We were raising four children in a one-bedroom house. My husband had been sober only a short time in AA and was still struggling to keep an automobile salvage business going, but it was in bankruptcy.

One day, I was sorting clothes to take to the laundromat. The bedspread on our bed was so ragged that I decided to throw it away because it wasn't worth washing again. Shortly afterward, my husband pulled in an old junk car with a beautiful off-white George Washington-style bedspread in it.

He brought it to the house and asked me if it was worth washing. I said, "Yes, it is." When my husband left (just to show you how ungrateful I had become), I looked at the bedspread and thought, "Darn! Why couldn't it have been a pink bedspread to go with the blue bedroom walls?" And I continued to sort clothes.

In about 20 minutes, my husband pulled in another junk car, and I know this is hard to believe, but he walked in with the most beautiful pink bedspread you ever laid eyes on. It looked like someone had just taken it out of the package.

My husband said, "Honey, could you use another bedspread?" I could hardly get the words out, "Well, yes."

When he left, I went into the bedroom, folded my hands, and looked up to a God that I didn't believe in and said, "Please, God, don't send me any more bedspreads. I've got all I need."

This was truly the beginning of my belief in the spiritual nature of the program. I had heard about such happenings from people around the tables, but it wasn't until I experienced it myself that I could really relate to it. I do believe that the Higher Power will go to any lengths to let us know He loves and cares for us. For those of us who aren't blessed with the "gift of faith," this Higher Power sometimes seems to perform miracles in a physical or material way so that we can believe.

Elsewhere in the same book, it says, "Faith does not remain automatically in the mind." I must be constantly reminded of what I believe in. To reinforce my faith, my belief, I need to keep seeking. I do this through daily contact with my sponsor, reading Conference Approved Literature, regular attendance at Al-Anon meetings and, last but not least, through prayer and meditation with God as I understand Him.

I can sum up my feelings with something I heard or read somewhere in this program. "I thank God for giving me Al-Anon, and I thank Al-Anon for giving me God."

—Missouri, United States

Having heard about "spiritual experiences" in Step Twelve and elsewhere, I wanted spiritual experience with rushing and a bright light, and I began to read about them. But the more I learned about spiritual experiences, the more I came to believe that you probably had to be in the depths of despair before you could have one. I sure hoped that to have one, I wouldn't have to suffer as I had already, for I had been depleted spiritually, mentally and physically when I came into Al-Anon five years before. So I put off wanting to have a spiritual experience because of this fear.

Then one night, I was camping on a beautiful beach and couldn't sleep, so I went for a walk and gazed up at the sky. One star seemed to get very bright and when I stopped and looked at it, it appeared to become larger and brighter and began to move toward me. I looked at it for some time, as it increased into a magnificent shining white light and continued gliding toward me. I thought, "'I'm going to have my spiritual experience. I can't just be struck down here on this expanse of beach all by myself. What if I am hit, like lightning strikes people? Nobody will find me until morning." Becoming frightened, I ran into the woods so that I couldn't see the light. I decided that I didn't have the courage to go through with a spiritual experience.

Early one Sunday morning, a year later I was in church, sitting near the front. The sun beamed through the beautiful stained glass window over the altar, and the muted rainbow of colors shone directly down on me. I began to feel tingly all over and thought, "I'm going to have my spiritual experience right here before all these people. What if I fall back and start convulsing or something? I don't want to do anything spectacular like that in front of everybody!" I slid over, out of the beautiful glow, and looked down, avoiding it. Now, I really put having a spiritual experience out of my mind because I had twice been so terrified when I thought one was coming.

Several years passed, and one night I was alone in a motel room lying on the bed. I began to have a feeling of leaving my body. I stayed right there, in the room, but I was just thoughts with no body. I began a dialogue, silently, with someone or something not myself. I have no idea of its gender, tone, or shape, but the voice was clear and spoke in English. I felt clean and cool. I communicated my concerns silently, and we discussed each in turn. No matter what degree of seriousness I placed on individual concerns, each was treated equally.

The end result of each discussion was that everything would work out; no matter what trouble I thought I had, it really wasn't trouble. It was just like a passage of time, with no good or bad value placed on it. I could see that my life was all right, that I didn't have to plan beyond any event and that each incident in life is important. The present is what matters. Then, right after my thoughts returned to my body, I felt I could transcend everyday upsets from now on and live with the same spiritual tranquillity I had been experiencing. To do this, all I had to do was believe as I did then: that every event in my life, no matter what importance I placed upon it, is spiritual, as is my mind. I experienced a great freedom. There was no fear, no concern, no tenseness, just a tranquil mental and emotional calm, a peaceful expectancy of existence.

Later, my roommate returned, and we talked

about the events of the day. I had no desire to share my experience. But I felt different—excited and alive with a conscienceness I had never felt before. I went to sleep, grateful that I had experienced a spiritual awakening. I awoke with the same feeling and just did the things I normally would do. The feeling began to melt away about midmorning, and I have never again experienced a spiritual feeling that intense.

What is different about me for having had a longed-for spiritual experience? I have a greater sense of well-being, yet new character defects come and some old ones continue. I am able to remember the experience and my feelings in detail, but I can't relive it, nor have I tried to. I no longer have that totally cleansed feeling, but I do experience calmness and peace when I remember it. I feel that, just as I am grateful to Al-Anon for saving my mind, spirit and body, I am grateful to God for having let me experience wisdom once, even for a short time.

—*Florida, United States*

I held many things in my hands and lost them all, but whatever I placed in God's hands, I still possess.

—*South Carolina, United States*

5

Letting Go

Some of us are still awaiting a spiritual awakening; others have experienced the profound changes described in the last chapter. But we are still human, regardless of our spiritual condition, and it takes daily effort on our part to make spiritual progress. One of the most difficult areas for many members of Al-Anon is control.

For years before we found the program, we spent much of our time trying to control the alcoholics and non-alcoholics in our lives. By the time we found Al-Anon, many of us had become bitter, angry, resentful and frustrated at our inability to make any changes in the behavior of others. Yet, many of us had a very difficult time letting go of our outdated beliefs: that we were doing or had done something wrong; that we could have or should have stopped the drinking. Despite our repeated failures in the past, many of us still felt responsible for other people's thinking and behavior. In many cases, these feelings were reinforced by alcoholic behavior. When we came to Al-Anon, we were told that we were only responsible for our contributions to the situation, not for the alcoholism itself.

In this chapter, we are concerned with the process of "Letting Go and Letting God." Many of us have heard the newcomer ask, "How long does it take to regain trust in myself, in the alcoholic and in God?" The answer is that this is usually a gradual process. If we attend meetings, read our Al-Anon literature, talk to other members, and "act as if" we believe, one day we discover that we can Let Go and Let God without worrying about the outcome. For many of us, that is one of the most liberating aspects of Al-Anon. We no longer have to carry the heavy burdens alone because we have a Higher Power to help us.

The differences between Step Three and Step Eleven may not be readily apparent, but for most of us, a considerable period of time elapses between turning ourselves over to the care of God and turning the everyday trivialities of life over to His care. For a time, we seem to reserve certain areas of our lives for our own control. Experience in the Al-Anon program, however, eventually teaches us that surrender of all areas of our lives will lead to freedom, happiness, and a peace of mind that was unimaginable to us before Al-Anon.

This letter was written by an Al-Anon member to another member who was hospitalized in a mental hospital after a suicide attempt.

Dear J.,

Tears filled my eyes as I read the account of your attempt to take your own life. As you described in your letter the years since we last met, I felt your hurt and despair.

I remember when you were married and how you began to have so many bruises. You tell me now that your husband would get drunk and beat you, and you would feel humiliated and so deeply hurt within. You must have felt sadly alone, since you were unable to share this burden with anyone. I know from your letter that you now realize he was sick, miserable and suffering from a disease over which he had no control. You are wise to realize that you, too, were lacking spiritual and emotional maturity.

I understand your feelings of guilt and depression when you think about the times of screaming and arguing and fighting and the ridiculous things you did and said. But you did the best you were capable of doing at the time. Today, you can grow toward becoming more emotionally stable, looking backward only in order to learn from your mistakes and to remember the good times. Yesterday can ruin today only if we let it; we can live and enjoy and be grateful for today.

The sense of worthlessness that you describe is not unusual in the spouse of an alcoholic. It's not that the drinker is responsible for this feeling, but that feelings such as these are nurtured by two very sick people on a merry-go-round, each powerless to get out of the cycle of madness without the help of a Power greater than themselves.

How sad it is that you feel so unloved and unwanted. When you begin to attend the Al-Anon meetings at the hospital, you will learn that you are loved and that people are deeply concerned about you. The people you meet there will understand as no one else can about the anger and contempt you feel . . . and the loneliness.

Remember how we used to talk about the fact that we couldn't really understand the Higher Power of the universe? It was only after I had reached a state of spiritual bankruptcy that I was able to admit that I was completely powerless over anyone's drinking and that I was doing a poor job of managing my life. I came to believe that He could restore me to better mental health and made a decision to turn my will and my life over to Him completely. Today, I have faith that things will continue to get better for me, day by day, sometimes without my realizing that it's happening.

I share my experience, my strength, and my hope with you because I love you and I love the Al-Anon program. This program of living will provide you with tools for recovery and growth. It's up to you how much you make use of the tools.

—*Louisiana, United States*

I don't need to understand the Power greater than myself, only to trust it.
—*New Jersey, United States*

I thought that I was working my Al-Anon program fairly well on my own initiative, but working with God was a different story. I found it difficult to let go, even though He has given me some miracles to boost my faith. I am still too powerful for my own good because I'm afraid of losing control and I don't want to trust anyone, even God, to help me. After encouragement from friends, I eventually took a chance and "tried some trust." It took time before I saw any results but it helped me develop the motivation to work my program more deeply and to learn to trust.
—*Anonymous*

The idea of faith and trust can be illustrated in a little story about a highwire act. The acrobat stands on a platform far above the crowd and asks if they believe he can walk the 40-foot high wire to the other platform. The audience responds; he crosses over successfully, and they applaud.

Next, he stands poised to push a wheelbarrow across and asks if they have faith he can do it. They cheer him on and applaud again.

Then he asks who has enough trust to climb into the wheelbarrow while he pushes it across the wire!

We need enough trust in our Higher Power to climb into His wheelbarrow only one day, one performance, at a time.

—*California, United States*

When I came into Al-Anon, I was very confused. I was unable to concentrate on anything except my husband's drinking. It was hard for me to understand what people in the program tried to tell me; I could only latch onto the simplest things. But from my very first meeting, I felt the love and fellowship.

They told me, "First Things First. You are the most important person in your life. If you'll put yourself and this program first, the things you're worrying about will be taken care of." I worried about a lot of things in those days: my husband's sobriety, my oldest son's chest pains (so severe nothing would stop them), my daughter's stomach pains (so bad she couldn't walk), my sanity, the utility bills, money for groceries, laundry and a million other things. So I began to try to put myself and this program first. I made sure I got back to that meeting every week, come hell or high water!

They told me to put First Things First: get myself in shape mentally and spiritually by asking for help from my Higher Power at the beginning of each day. When I could overcome my pride and begin to do this, the days began to go better for myself and the children, even though my husband continued to drink.

My sponsor told me that my health and my children's came first because I was responsible for them while they were young. We were the only ones I could take care of right now. Believe it or not, I didn't know that until she told me!

After a time, I began to see that all the things I worried about were taken care of. My son's chest pains and my daughter's stomach pains disappeared. Could it be I had caused them by my nervousness, nagging and complaining? When the water, lights and gas were cut off (as they were several times), my husband, even in his drunken state, still found a way to get them turned back on. Somehow there was always enough money. It was never a lot, just "enough." And most miraculously of all, after I had been in the program a couple of years, my husband became sober!

I believe that all these blessings, and many more, are the result of putting First Things First—myself and this program—and leaving room for God to work His miracles.

—*Missouri, United States*

A few years ago, my father was in the hospital dying of cancer, and I was trying to be a source of support for my mother. I had accepted my father's inevitable death. I didn't want him to live if he couldn't be out in his garden and visit his cabin on the river as he loved to do. My concern was to help my mother, and I hadn't yet turned this responsibility over to my Higher Power.

At one point, I had been visiting my mother for a while and needed to return to my family for a few days. On the flight back, we made a few stops in smaller towns to pick up passengers. As we approached one of these towns, the pilot announced that the winds were rather strong, so we had to remain at a higher altitude and make a steeper descent than usual. He assured us that everything would be okay.

I sat there wishing my Higher Power, like the pilot, would make an announcement and tell me exactly what was going to happen, when it was going to happen and how it was going to turn out. I sat and thought about this for what seemed like a long time, and then I realized that we wouldn't need faith if we knew what was going to happen ahead of time.

A few weeks later, after I had gone to bed, I told God that my mother was getting awfully tired and I didn't know how much longer she would be able to visit the hospital every day. At midnight, the phone rang and it was the hospital calling to say that my father died. At first, I felt a little guilty, thinking that perhaps I was responsible for his death, but soon I knew that God had answered a prayer that had not really asked for anything. I had just given Him the problem for His solution.

This experience was a faith-builder for me. Through Al-Anon, I now try to take my problems to my Higher Power, but I leave the solutions and the timetable up to Him.

—*Nebraska, United States*

When it comes to big decisions, loss of a loved one, or serious personal or family problems, I trust that if I do my part, the Higher Power will do the rest. The everyday fears are another matter.

One evening, I was planning to speak at an Al-Anon meeting. My sober husband, some Al-Anon friends and I all left the house at the same time. My husband said he would walk the few blocks to get the car at the gas station. Years ago, that would have been an excuse to stop off to drink. Those thoughts never entered my mind until I happened to see him walking toward the local firehouse where he used to drink. Just as I saw him, my friends stopped the car at the corner and asked me which way to turn. If I told them to turn right, I could check up on him, but I answered, "Turn left," and began to share my fear.

One friend said that through Al-Anon she had learned that the old fears can come back no matter how long or how hard we have worked the program. It's up to us how we use the tools of Al-Anon to overcome the fears. As I listened, I realized I had choices. I began to silently share these with my Higher Power. I could allow the old feelings to take over and let the fear ruin my evening; or I could trust that whatever might happen to my husband was in the hands of the Higher Power and that would help me have faith in myself, my husband, the program, and even to have enough faith in the Higher Power to let go of the fear.

I was the second speaker at the meeting. I listened to the first speaker with a serenity that only comes to me when I really work the Al-Anon program. When it was my turn to speak, I never thought of my fear. I had shared it, turned it over, and it had been replaced by faith.

When I returned home, the fear also returned for a moment as I saw my husband on the couch, the place he always occupied after a night at the firehouse. This time, my Al-Anon friends were not there, but the Al-Anon principles were. I remembered to take a deep breath and turn it over to the Higher Power.

My husband opened his eyes and asked about my evening. He was sober, all my fears were groundless. He told me what a good feeling it was to have his old friends invite him to see the new fire engine and how much he enjoyed being there sober.

I felt good, too. I shared how I felt when I saw him go toward the firehouse, pointing out that that is how my disease can recur and admitting how hard it is to work the program at times like that.

I was successful in overcoming my fear because I used the Al-Anon tools. That night I felt the peaceful feeling that comes to me when I work at my faith—in myself, the Higher Power, and Al-Anon.

—*Anonymous*

I understand that I need a positive attitude and that I have to work the Eleventh Step. To change my attitude, I have to let go and abandon the steering wheel of my ship, refusing to let others disturb me or make me feel unhappy. To keep my serenity, I have to understand and practice acceptance. I have to let my Higher Power take charge of the problem. I have to let go of everything without holding back the smallest part.

—*Quebec, Canada*

"Yes, but if you lived in my situation, you'd understand why I'm so miserable. If I had everything you had (or looked the way you do, or didn't have to . . .), I'd be happy, too."

On the surface, this statement is understandable and human. We tend to agree because some circumstances seem unfair, are more difficult and do require more coping; and there are some people who do seem to "have it made."

Until I faced this hidden belief, I continued to think I had a deep faith in God and denied that I was agnostic in some areas of my life. I discovered that I believed in God, but did not believe He would help in any way with my current problem.

This admission shocked me so much that I

immediately prayed, "Of course I believe you love me and will take care of . . ." The words fell flopping to the floor, and I knew I was lying. So I started over and asked to be willing to believe.

After admitting this to my sponsor, I could start "acting as if" I believed, by behaving the way I wanted to become. That made it okay, not a lie anymore, because she and God knew why my behavior didn't match my feelings yet. By this process I was changed and I came to believe.

When I believe in His power, I can make the decision to live (with God's help) a reasonably happy, serene life. This does not mean I walk around glowing all the time. (I might even have to remove myself from a situation temporarily or permanently.) But it does give me a place to start over when I think, "I could be happy if . . ."
—*Texas, United States*

I have lived in all-consuming fear the majority of my life. Change terrified me. Through this program and the people in it, God has healed me with His touch of pure, unchangeable love so that I am able to adjust to ever-changing relationships. With this flexibility, fear takes a minor role, and faith and trust are now a major part of my life.

This program of "know thyself" has enabled me to become aware of the "alarm bells" of the negatives. Awareness is so much better for me than closing out all feelings, shutting out people, withdrawing from living. No matter how hard the truth is or what the facts are, I prefer to know, look at and accept this day. This is preferable to mere existence, and I believe that living in fear is just existing.

With faith and trust in a Higher Power, love is replacing that fear. Trust, compassion, stability— the things I have hungered for all my life—allow me to have choices. I can experience being alive. I no longer have to crawl subserviently, but can stand tall and walk straight with love, peace, serenity and faith in God.

Fear is finally something I can acknowledge and deal with directly. It is not the controlling

factor in my life. I refuse to let it be that way anymore. Al-Anon has shown me another way of living, and I like it. Life can either be a burden and
a chore or a challenge and a joy. One Day at a
Time I can meet the challenges of life head-on
instead of headdown.

—*Venezuela*

While watering the trees one afternoon, I used
the most water on a tree that had died the year
before. I was trying so hard to revive it.

My son came out and asked, "Mother, why are
you wasting so much of that precious stuff on
that tree? God's the only one who can help it
now."

At that moment that tree was my husband just
as plain as day, and I had been wasting all my
"precious stuff" on him and his drinking, when
God was the only one who could help him now.
For the first time, I finally understood release.
What a blessing that has been!

—*Texas, United States*

Before Al-Anon, I believed in a Higher Power I chose to call God. Whenever I needed help, He was there. But when it came to my husband, the alcoholic in my life, I had a blind spot because I thought that, as a good wife, it was my responsibility to get him to stop drinking. I prayed to God to give me the words to get him to stop drinking. For some reason, I had a need to be God's instrument.

I just kept digging and digging because somewhere I was sure I'd find the answer. In reality, I was digging a big hole for myself, and finally I hit bedrock. I felt I was down so deep that my Higher Power couldn't hear my voice anymore. I couldn't trust God, my husband, not even myself. I was filled with despair.

Then things got even worse: my husband was in trouble at work, and there was the possibility he would lose his job. With five young children, it seemed to be the end. I went to church that Sunday, and my soul cried out, "Help him." I surrendered.

In a few days, his employer gave him an ultimatum of going into a rehabilitation center or being fired. He admitted for the first time that he had a problem and went without a murmur. And I was resentful because I had not been the one to convince him to go. But I began to realize that the God of my understanding works through people.

I began to trust my Higher Power. Oh, it was hard because I would turn things over, then take them back. But through Steps Three and Eleven I learned and grew. In Al-Anon, I began to trust others as I listened and learned. As my self-esteem grew, I learned to trust myself to make judgments and decisions. As my husband became sober and grew in his program, I began to trust him once more.

The God of my understanding is loving and kind, ready to help me. I have only to ask, and He is there to show me the way. It may not be the answer I *want*, but I have to remember that it may be what I *need*. I must remember just to trust.

—*New Jersey, United States*

Through study and practice by myself and with my group, Al-Anon helped bring back to the surface the spiritual values hidden deep down inside me. They had been squelched by my inability to see, hear or feel life. I just functioned. I had nearly allowed myself to lose my spiritual values because of anger, resentments, fears and frustrations.

But, because our program is totally spiritual, Al-Anon gave me the courage to start mending my life. With a closer contact with my Higher Power, I began appreciating life and enjoying it.

The Twelve Steps and Twelve Traditions don't even mention the word "love," but by using them, I find that a new expression of love has come into my life. It helps me accept things the way they are. It also helps me to concentrate on my life and to Let Go and Let God handle those problems I can do nothing to correct.

—*Anonymous*

Before Al-Anon, I was filled with fears—

some justified, others the figments of my imagination. I feared many things that never materialized. By using the Al-Anon tools in my personal recovery, living the program as it slowly unfolded, and practicing the Twelve Steps as honestly as I could, I gradually overcame some of my fears.

Sometimes I would falter and fears would return. So I used the Serenity Prayer. I really opened up to my Higher Power, whom I choose to call God. Sometimes I would phone an Al-Anon friend and talk it over. Knowing that I am not alone helps me gain perspective. I learned that just for today, I will not be afraid; just for this moment, I will not be afraid. Many, many times I cut my day into small segments: "Dear God, please help me through the next few minutes." I would sit quietly, confident in His power, and soon I would feel God's hand at work.

Fear is natural and it takes courage, faith and honesty to look within so that as fears lessen, we can begin to concentrate on ourselves and thus find emotional security and spiritual peace. Calmness and trying to live one day at a time in a rational way enable me to face whatever comes, and I can accept God's will for me. My solace and assurance is in the knowledge that God is constant, a never-ending source of guidance and wisdom. He is always there if I seek Him.

—*Canada*

I was walking in the woods one day. A few weeks earlier, a tornado had come through the area. I walked into the forest as far as I could safely go, then sat down on one of the fallen trees. All around me, huge, old trees were uprooted. It reminded me of the pick-up sticks game I played when I was a child. Sitting there, I felt small and powerless, and I realized how truly powerful God is. And I remembered how, in the past, I had struggled so long and hard, thinking I could handle everything on my own. I tried everything I could think of to get the alcoholic to stop drinking. So much of my time was spent thinking of him that I lost a lot of years when my two children were young. I can't even remember some of those years.

Sitting there looking at the destruction, I wondered how I could ever have thought that God couldn't help me. I realized that I had never allowed Him to help me. I was incapable of letting go and letting God. My life had to become a real mess, like the forest, before I could see the importance of allowing God in. The destruction also showed me the importance of living one day at a time and not missing any of the beauty around me.

I'm grateful God has given me this awareness. It's been a long and lonely road, but it was necessary for me. And with God's guidance, it's one road I won't be traveling again.

—*New York, United States*

Sometimes, we try so hard that we fail to see that the light we are seeking is within us and that God is with us and is the answer to our needs.

Very early in the Al-Anon program, we are told to "Let Go and Let God." This does not mean that we will do nothing. It simply means that we will let God work through us to give expression to perfect ideas and constructive thoughts. To know this and accept it as the truth enables us to be free and to be at peace in mind and body. I've seen this work in my own group. Where there is peace, there has to be love, and only when we "Let Go and Let God" can we feel this inner peace.

—*South Carolina, United States*

My husband has now been sober for eight years. We run our business together, and life is good. When he was new in AA, although he was getting better, he was unable to keep his sobriety or a job for very long. Even so, sobriety always brought hope for the future and new plans for continued sobriety.

When he managed to get a job as a boiler attendant at the local hospital, he had great hopes and plans. But he picked up that first drink, and I was terribly worried when I came home from work one day to find him drunk. It soon became apparent that he intended to go to the liquor store to get more liquor to take to work with him. He was due to start work at 11:00 p.m., and I was appalled at the thought of his being in charge of an electric boiler in that condition. I was afraid he would pass out and blow the hospital, its patients and staff sky-high! So I talked to him. He was too drunk to answer, but I chattered on, talking about this and that, to hold him there until the store closed at 10:00 p.m., so that he could not get there to buy more liquor.

I talked; I watched the clock to see how long I would have to hold him. Suddenly, the thought came: "Just a minute! This is not letting go and letting God!" I was shocked. I knew that I must stop talking and start trusting the Higher Power. So I stopped talking. Relieved, my husband left. I went into my bedroom, got down on my knees and prayed. I spent the whole night praying, wondering what was happening and worrying. I wanted to phone his boss, someone in authority at the hospital, or someone in Al-Anon, but I was afraid he would lose his job no matter what I did or who I called. Then I would remember to turn once again to my Higher Power in prayer, but the fear of the newspaper headlines was never far from the surface. I could visualize the explosion and the mangled bodies.

Miraculously, when my husband arrived home, he had been shocked into sobriety. His boss, who had never visited him on the job, had been out to the theater and decided to stop in and say hello. One look at a drunken man trying to pour another drink, spilling more on the floor than into the glass, made him look toward the dials and jump into action.

Amazingly, the boiler indicated that it was past the point where it should have blown. The needle was jammed down as far as it would go, yet it hadn't blown!

Although he lost his job, the shock of realizing what he almost did was enough to start him working his AA program in earnest. And the

experience of that night was enough to make me remember to "Let Go and Let God."
—*Australia*

If I can grasp the concept of "Let Go and Let God," anyone can! I was very independent and self-reliant; I was a domineering perfectionist. I was also agnostic. In other words, I was a godless, hard-boiled person. So, to find in this fellowship that I was allowed to be dependent and compliant, to make mistakes, and to find a Higher Power who would lead and guide me was a miracle.

I had to turn my God-given free will, my self-determination—in other words, myself— over to my Higher Power and allow him to take the reins and to guide me in all aspects of my life. I could not do this once and then forget it. I have to do it at least once a day by prayer, meditation, and talking with my Higher Power on a one-to-one basis—in other words, by practicing Step Eleven.

It is not easy to stop worrying, meddling and rescuing. I started out by turning minor problems over to God and chanting to myself, "Let Go and Let God." Gradually, I worked my way up to the point where I can turn all other people, places and things over, without any doubts or qualms. To accomplish this takes time—it cannot be done at once—and it needs to be done on a continuing basis. In the same manner, I started working on myself. I started with little problems of my own and gradually learned to turn myself over to the care of God completely.

I can't say that I don't unconsciously snatch everything back periodically: I do, because I'm only human. But when I do grab it all back, everything starts to go wrong, and this wakes me up to what I've done, making me realize that I have to "Let Go and Let God."

Sometimes letting go requires loving people enough to let them go and allow them to fall flat on their faces without any interference from you. You can allow them to pick themselves up or stay down, whichever is their choice. This can be very painful, but the more often it is practiced, the easier it becomes. (It never becomes easy, but it hurts less each time.)

Still, having learned all this doesn't mean that I can sit back and twiddle my thumbs and do nothing. I have to continue to work the program, keeping my mind, heart, eyes and ears receptive to the Higher Power's guidance and enlightenment, which comes to us in a myriad of ways.

One evening, I returned home to find my husband sprawled on the bed. He was nearly naked, with no teeth, and skinny from days of not eating, just drinking and sleeping. He was most unlovely.

My heart sank as I looked at him, and I was filled with pity for myself, but not for him. He only filled me with despair. I knew that love was the answer, but I did not feel that I could love him anymore. Standing there looking at him, but not knowing what to do, I said to the God of my understanding, "God, I know you love him and I know that you want me to love him, but I cannot.

You will have to love him through me. Please love him through me."

I felt a force like an electric current flow from above and through my head, down through my body and out from the region of my heart toward that shrunken figure on the bed. I trembled with the force of its impact. It seemed to reach my husband also for he opened his eyes and saw me. I will never forget it. He looked into my eyes and he was looking for condemnation, abuse, anger, disgust, hate. But apparently all he could see was this wonderful love. He gave a trembly moan of thanks and said, "Thank you for coming back." Filled with awe at what I had experienced and anxious that he, too, realize it was the love of God that he was witnessing, I replied, "It is not me, I assure you. If it was up to me, I'd be miles away by now. Can't you see, it is a 'Power greater than ourselves'?"

This was just one more step in his path toward sobriety and my path toward obeying and loving my Higher Power.

—*Australia*

Though no one can go back and make a brand new start, anyone can start from now and make a brand new end.

—*Anonymous*

It was a strange thing. There was something funny going on. Every time I took a book off the shelf at the library, there would be a message in it, and the message was love. Each book would reinforce the message, even quote from other books, even though my selections were random. I asked myself how love was possible in my situation. My husband was reaching the end of his alcoholic road and there was no hope; we were doomed. I decided that I was just imagining the message.

Shortly afterward, a friend persuaded me to try Al-Anon. I had never heard of it, had no conception of what it could be, but because of her insistence, I finally attended a meeting. I knew at once that this was what I had been searching for. I saw glowing, happy people. I met recovering alcoholics, something I hadn't thought possible. I was filled with hope.

Before long, however, I started to slide into a strange depression. Each day it was worse. I told my sponsor, and she said, "This, too, shall pass." But it didn't; it became deeper. Suddenly one day, I was overcome by it. I seemed to fall into depths I had never experienced before and had a mental picture of my life as a total wasteland, a desert without a sign of life—bleak, dry and stony. And I felt that God wanted me to wipe it out. Looking at this grim picture, I could see no reason to continue living; my life seemed a total waste of time, and I began to believe that it was God's will for me to die. With all my strength, I called to Him, "God, help me!"

At that very moment, the phone rang and my doctor asked me for the name of a specialist in alcoholism, and I was able to blurt out that I thought I needed to see a psychiatrist right away. So I went to see one, but after three visits, he said I didn't need him because all I had done every time was tell him how wonderful Al-Anon was.

A few days later, I heard a voice behind me. It said, "You are accepted." There was nothing else; I couldn't understand it. Accepted by whom? For what? What was expected of me? There was no answer to my wonder-filled questions.

A few days after that, I became aware of a presence beside me as I was doing the dishes. I saw nothing, but my mind was gripped in a way that seemed like somebody tapping me on the shoulder and saying, "Pay attention." And I was surrounded, enclosed, lapped in the most glorious sensation of being loved, comforted, warmed, held securely. It is impossible to describe it.

A voice spoke. I heard it on the right side of me, not at all like when you run a conversation in your head; I heard it through my ear. And the voice told me that everything would be all right, that my marriage was important and I must do everything in my power to strengthen it, that love was the most important thing in the world;

187

indeed, that the universe ran on love. And I could see that it was so. The voice teased me, laughed at me in a loving way, told me that all the things in my life that I thought of as sins were just mistakes, mistakes in living. Finally, the voice told me that present joy wipes out all past unhappiness. And so I have found it to be.

Having taken the Twelve Steps in all sincerity and to the best of my ability, I believe that I did have the spiritual awakening that is promised in the Twelfth Step. I have therefore endeavored to carry this message to others in the ensuing thirteen years, and intend to continue to do so, One Day at a Time, to the end of my life.

—*Australia*

When we feel the absence of God, remember, He hasn't moved.

—*New York, United States*

6

Prayer and Meditation

For every concept of a "Higher Power" mentioned in the last chapter, there is a corresponding approach to prayer, meditation, and achieving a conscious contact with the "God of our understanding." The importance of practicing Step Eleven is emphasized by a member from New Zealand: "All people who achieve, practice. I had received freedom through a spiritual awakening and daily practice was the only way to keep this freedom."

Many of us did not learn how to pray and meditate until we had come to terms with our own definitions of a Power greater than ourselves. For those of us who were prone to analyze every aspect of our lives before we could take action, praying required a gigantic leap of faith: the belief that something or someone was listening. And we needed to feel comfortable with our concept of God. Once we accepted this, we could pray, believing that it would work for us; and we experienced for ourselves the profound changes that resulted from it. Our experiences with prayer have confirmed that intellectual acceptance of the concept of prayer is meaningless. True knowledge of its power to transform our lives can only be gained through practice; "knowledge without action is fantasy."

For many of us, meditation was even more difficult to define and practice than was prayer. Many of our prayers were said in times of desperation and turmoil; yet, they were answered nonetheless. But meditation required deliberate action and at least minimal calm. Many of us had never even attempted meditation before and were unsure of how to do it and wondered if it was really worthwhile.

Here we found that ignorance was not necessarily a disadvantage. We could achieve satisfaction through our halting attempts because our "conscious contact with God" was better than it had ever been before. And Step Eleven tells us that our purpose is to improve that contact. We sought "progress, not perfection."

For most of us, the search for a more satisfying method of meditation continues until we find something we are comfortable doing. And we continue in that practice as long as it gives us new insights into our lives because we have learned that most growth is gained by living through it, by tackling our problems, and by allowing ourselves to be transformed by the love of Al-Anon and the love of our Higher Power. Improving our conscious contact on a daily basis renews our faith and strengthens our resolve to live in peace One Day at a Time.

This chapter explores the variety of approaches which are used by Al-Anon members to achieve that end.

After many years of living with active alcoholism, I was fortunate enough to be introduced to Al-Anon, and although it took me a long time to understand what it was all about, in time I began to Listen and Learn, to work the Steps and live the program. I had the benefit of the Al-Anon program for nearly eight years before my husband passed away. I was able to thank God that He had at last removed the terrible burden of alcoholism from my husband, and I found peace and a release in knowing that my husband would no longer suffer. By this time, Al-Anon had become my way of life and I didn't even consider whether I still needed it; I just kept coming to meetings and I received a great deal of comfort from my program and my Al-Anon friends.

After a couple of years, I met a sober alcoholic, an AA member, and we started dating. He had been through two marriages and did not intend to marry again. This was fine with me; marriage hadn't been too kind to me either. As our friendship progressed, we realized that we had come to care deeply for each other, so we decided to live together without marrying. It was not an easy decision; my generation did not do things like that; I would be setting a bad example for my grandchildren; people would not approve. After much soul-searching, however, we decided to go ahead.

We were very happy, but I still had reservations. Feeling that I was sinning against God, I prayed for forgiveness. I tried to point out to God in my prayers that it was better for two people who loved each other to live together in happiness than to be miserable separately. I also prayed that, if God couldn't forgive us for this sin, He might make it possible for us to marry. It wasn't long before my partner quite casually asked one day if I would like to get married, and I learned that he was just as troubled about our relationship as I was. I didn't give him a chance to change his mind! We were married a week later with the good wishes and joy of our families and our fellowship friends.

I wish I could end this story saying that we lived happily ever after, but I can't. We had been married less than a year and had been very happy when my husband was involved in a traffic accident in which a pedestrian was killed. Although he was absolved of all blame, this dreadful experience plunged him into a deep depression. His program and friends helped him, but he had a very hard time accepting what had happened. Al-Anon had taught me that I was not responsible, that I should detach from the problem, but I slipped badly and went right down into the depths of despair with him. I know now that it is not for me to question God's plan for us. I pray to my Higher Power, and instead of asking Him why this had to happen, I ask that I may learn acceptance. I know that I have to accept this, but I am powerless to do anything about it. My partner has to deal with it in his own way with the benefit of his program. I will continue to give him my love and support, but that is all I can do.

I am in the habit of taking long walks every morning, and I use that time to meditate and talk to God. I pray to remember to be grateful. I thank God for the happy years of my childhood in a loving home and for the early years of my first marriage, when our children were small and the drinking had not yet become a problem. And I thank Him for the drinking years, too, because without them I would never have found Al-Anon and learned the process of growing up. I thank God also for the good relationship I have with my grown children. I pray that they may be given the strength and courage to face whatever befalls them in life, and I thank God for giving me a second chance at happiness with a loving gentle person. If we each work our individual programs, we can make it with God's help.

—*Canada*

In Al-Anon, I learned that God meets me where I am. I don't have to rearrange myself or become "good" enough before I can approach Him. If I am just willing, He will come to me. He has not chosen to make His will known to me in neon lights, so I often pray that He will show me if my actions are not in harmony with His will.

My commitment to Step Eleven includes making time to work on this relationship with my Higher Power. During my daily quiet time, I try to focus all my attention on God. When I take my problems to Him, I try to leave them there and keep my focus of attention on Him. In working this Step, I have come to believe that God usually does not send a crisis nor take it away, but that He gives me the grace I need to turn a crisis into an opportunity for growth. In this Step, I have come to know gratitude, serenity, joy and peace.

—*Texas, United States*

One evening I was writing my daily inventory and pouring out my despair in dealing with a certain area of my life. In a written prayer at the end, I realized that I was right in the middle of the Sixth and Seventh Steps, telling my Higher Power that I was entirely ready to have Him remove this problem and humbly asking Him to do for me what I could not do for myself.

Incredibly, the response was immediate; the compulsive behavior I had struggled with for years was removed. And in a moment of clarity, I saw that this Step does not say we "were entirely ready to have God help us remove these defects of character." It says we "were entirely ready to have God remove all these defects of character."

I continued to ask for His help each day of the following week, and each day the problem was removed. Then the day came when I took the situation back into my own hands, and my Higher Power allowed me the right to do so. Once again, I experienced the despair and pain that come from acting on my own self-will. The struggle continued over a period of time as I alternately surrendered and took control again until I was, indeed, "entirely ready."

This problem and many others are being removed on a daily basis by a Power greater than myself, who asks only that I remain willing to have Him act in my life. And today I express that willingness by getting down on my knees in the morning and asking His help for that day and listening for His answers.

—*California, United States*

I know that I must work diligently to pray and meditate each day, regardless of my emotional or spiritual state, because if a crisis comes, self-pity and hopelessness are looming in the shadows. It would be very easy for me to succumb to old patterns of trying to control the events in my life and feeling frustrated at my inability to do so. I must turn "my life and my will" over to my Higher Power each day, for I have proved to myself that when I try to control the universe nothing goes my way, but when I "turn it over," miraculously, all areas of my life become acceptable, even pleasant. My life today is peaceful and calm, and I feel optimistic about the future. This is solely because I believe that "God is doing for me what I could not do for myself."

I never thought that I could conceptualize God in such a way. I never believed in divine intervention before I became a member of Al-Anon. But today, I not only believe in divine intervention, I feel that I am living proof of it. And I thank my Higher Power whenever I think to do so. Usually, I remember to thank God for my life, my program and my beautiful marriage before I get out of bed in the morning and before I go to sleep at night. And, during the day, whenever I realize that I have "handled a situation which used to baffle me," I say, "Thank you, God." I know that it is only this program and God's intervention that have given me the beautiful life I have today.

I am still uncomfortable about describing the changes in my life to others, particularly potential Al-Anon members. These changes are so profound and so all-encompassing that I am afraid I sound like a fanatic—and I am suspicious of fanaticism in others. But I try to carry the message by living life to the fullest and remaining constantly conscious of the source of all goodness and life, thanking Him/Her for the goodness that is my life today.

—*Indiana, United States*

When we turn to God, we find He has been facing us all the time.

—*Kansas, United States*

Our back door opens onto a three-by-five piece of cement that is gradually becoming an important part of my life. It is there that I have my lunch on the nice days of spring, summer, and fall, and where, in the early morning, I sometimes kneel in appreciation for the good I feel in my life. It is also there that I receive help to ease any inner pain which seems to be lingering.

My stoop faces south and one morning I realized that I always turned to my left to pray, facing east. Often the sun is so bright that it is physically uncomfortable to keep that position, and yet, to turn away in another direction seems equally uncomfortable.

It occurred to me that my way to God is in one direction, painful at times, but if I want Him in my life, I can't turn away.

This back stoop has nourished me—mentally, physically and spiritually.

—*New York, United States*

Save a time for silence in your day.

—*New Hampshire, United States*

I have found the value of consistency in prayer and meditation. It is not the quantity of time I spend in prayer; it is the quality. A few minutes every day is much better than a half hour every week. This really works for me: I

have fewer ups and downs in my program and
am less depressed.
—*British Columbia, Canada*

God is only a prayer away.
—*Illinois, United States*

How greatly my prayers have changed since I
came into Al-Anon! In my pre-Al-Anon days, I
prayed long, earnest, nightly prayers, enlisting
God's intervention in my husband's drinking,
enumerating the ways he needed to be changed
and naming all "my" children, relatives, and
friends, listing my solutions for their problems.
There were long, mournful recitations of my
own troubles and woes. God surely must have
been bored by my tedious repetitions!

I have loved and been involved in this program of Al-Anon for 22 years, and as the years
have passed, my prayers have changed greatly.
They have become much shorter and more fre-

quent. My first conscious contact comes before I get out of bed in the early morning. Because it is so early, I am able to distinguish the very first light of the day filtering through the trees and just barely across my window sill, and I think, "You are sending me another day . . . a new, fresh day!" And gratitude wells up inside me. Before getting out of bed, I take a Third Step, turning my will and my life over to His care; this is prayer to me. Then, if I will recall throughout the day that I am in His care, and I am expected to do my best and not try to force my own solutions, my day usually goes well.

My earnest prayer is that He will let me know His will for me in ways that I can understand. And I do hear and can understand . . . through a new understanding of a phrase in the literature or a bird's sweet call, through the eyes of a child in its mother's grocery cart, in the joy of answering the phone to "Hi, Mom!" or in the humble feeling when a struggling newcomer says, "Will you be my sponsor?" I know that He has communicated with me when I drag to a meeting, tired to the bone, but come home feeling elated and enthusiastic because the meeting seemed made to answer my immediate needs.

The last prayer of my day comes as I fall into bed. The words are always different, but the thought is the same: "How can I ever tell You of my boundless gratitude for all these joys and blessings, the comfort and strength brought to me by this Al-Anon way to live! But most of all, I am grateful for the awareness that You were with me this day!"

—*Georgia, United States*

I have gone through various methods of praying and have now settled for just thanking God for my blessings. When I used to make specific requests, I was so busy waiting for them to be granted that I didn't realize the answers were staring me in the face.

—*Anonymous*

Fear does not go away because you want it to. But I have learned it can be dealt with in small segments— day, an hour, a minute, sometimes only for the seconds it takes to say the Serenity Prayer over and over. Hard to do? Yes. But it can be done. I finally learned to pray not to have the problem removed, even though that's what I wanted, but instead for the willingness to accept the situation, the strength to work at whatever I needed to do. I did not feel as though "everything was going to be all right"—I was still afraid. But the paralyzing fear was gone. God was doing for me what I could not do for myself.

—*Anonymous*

True wisdom starts with a heart full of faith, not a head full of facts.

—*New York, United States*

In the past, I said my childhood prayers and all the "God bless" lists that children make. As I grew older, these prayers changed to "gimmee" or bargaining prayers: "Please, God, help me to pass this exam"; "Don't let me get in trouble"; "Let me win that and I'll . . ."; "Help me get well."

Then, during the troubled years of my life and family break-up, my prayers became less childish and took on a noticeable trust and faith, born probably of desperation. "God, help me, I don't know what to do. Show me . . . I trust You to see me through."

Sometimes, my prayers reverted back full-cycle as I tried to maintain contact with my Higher Power through prayers of adoration, confession, thanksgiving and petition. Finally, I have reached a point in my spiritual growth in which I pray for guidance to do and be whatever is required of me today. Thus, I'm learning to be happy and contented in my total relationship with my Higher Power.

In the morning, I try to do ten minutes of physical exercise to awaken properly; then I spend 10 to 20 minutes doing spiritual reading or meditation and praying for guidance to direct my heart and mind to the day's activities.

Now, I pray for the sake of praying. I try to put myself into my Higher Power's plans for me in a humble and trusting manner, trying to seek Him among my fellow travelers and to be ever alert to their cries. My prayers are becoming less noisy with more quiet listening. I try to see where I fit into His plans and where and how I can best serve His needs. I think I now understand what it means to "waste time with God," because it is in stopping and resting in Him that I get to know Him and His plans for me.

—*Saskatchewan, Canada*

A few years ago, I began to suspect that prayer was a response to God, that He initiated the relationship and my prayer simply acknowledged His presence and power. Then the committee in my head started asking questions; contradictions and paradoxes fought for admission to the discussion. "Ask and you shall receive . . . Be careful what you ask for, you might get it . . . Be specific, God cares about everything . . . Quit telling God what you want—He knows your needs better than you do."

With time, I learned to separate the ideas. "Be specific" has merits. Praying "forgive my sins" is vague and nothing changes, but when I recognize the power of naming a defect and asking for its removal or of naming a quality and asking for its enhancement, then—and only then—does change take place.

But why tell Him if He already knows? Because He wants me to know! My self-knowledge is never complete without interaction with God and another human being. When I eliminate God and others, I narrow my focus to self. When I focus on God, however, I find that He does the cleaning. He doesn't scrub so hard the paint comes off, or sweep one spot threadbare, or skimp on soap, or get mad if the phone rings, or forget to water the flowers. He doesn't sterilize my house into cold perfection. He just gently shows me what to polish, what to hold and enjoy, and what to clean. He helps me decorate my landscape with freshness.

I begin to see in a different way. In drawing, I have learned how a tree changes as I view it from different angles and distances, and how it changes as light moves through it, around it and to the other side. Funny how we can't see a shape when we look directly at it. We can't look directly at the sun, either, but to watch its light illuminate and define a tree is truly wonderful. Similarly, when I start to look at the space within which you live, at the light in your life, for the first time, I recognize your uniqueness and intricacy.

This is what the Eleventh Step has come to mean to me: watching the light and asking for the ability to see what is already planned, so that I will respond to the power instead of working against it.

Texas, United States

Complacency sets in if I take for granted the faith I have gained through this program. I become limited in my vision. I look at the visible things—people, trees, books, etc.—and I think that I gain strength from them. But visible things limit my awareness. The important things in life cannot be seen: acceptance, love, integrity, understanding. Yet I strive for these truths even though I am limited in my vision. Finding inner strength is looking beyond the visible and focusing life's search on the unseen.

My vision causes me to worry about the future because I cannot see what lies ahead. If such worries did not get in the way, I could spend more time realizing that the most important things are the invisible. As I concentrate more on the unseen, I become closer to my spiritual truth. God's will is invisible. I need to remember that to seek God's will I must strive to pay less attention to the visible and, instead, contemplate the invisible.

—*Alberta, Canada*

I am learning that if I wanted a drink of water, I would not go to the cupboard; if I were looking for a carpet, I would not go to the bakery. I must go to the source that supplies what I need. It wasn't until I stopped just saying the Serenity Prayer, and transferred it into my heart, that I saw it was giving me an important message about my search for serenity. It did not say, "children, grant me the serenity"; it did not say "partner, grant me serenity" nor "friends." It said God. And I came to realize that I had been looking for this precious commodity in the wrong places.

One Day at a Time, just for this day, I go to the source: God as I understand Him. I ask for my portion for this day, and only then can I be the sort of person I wouldn't mind being with for that day.

—*Australia*

The Serenity Prayer has become very meaningful to me. I no longer say it by rote. I think about it and try to mean what I am saying. I quit begging, pleading or bargaining. I came to believe the word "grant" means that all comes from and returns to God's hands. "Acceptance" means to accept my husband and remember that he loves me and that our marriage is working. I can't change yesterday, the drinking years, my teen years or my childhood, but I can learn from them. I can accept my co-workers and fellow Al-Anon members because they are all children of God, and it is not my place to judge them. "Courage" means that the only person I can change is me. Because my self-esteem and self-worth were so low, I need to remind myself constantly that I, too, am a child of God, that He loves me and wants what's best for me. Also, I ask for the courage to work on a specific defect, usually patience. "Wisdom" means learning the difference between my business and others' business.

I have also discovered another use for the Serenity Prayer; I use it as a daily inventory. By replacing the word "Grant" with "Thank You," I can review the day, learn from my mistakes, rec-

ognize His guidance, and give thanks.
—*Iowa, United States*

Oh, most potent source of comfort and strength, which I acknowledge but cannot define, grant me the wisdom to let my tears flow without shame whenever they are appropriate, the courage to love and to express my love in words and actions, and the serenity that comes when I can accept reality without trying to shape it to my expectations or my desires.
—*Anonymous*

In the past, when many bleak things were happening, if I remembered to pray, "God grant me the serenity . . . ," just saying "God" gave me instant release and serenity. I knew I wasn't alone, that I was surrounded by Him and by people whom He chose to speak to me. The terrible isolation of alcoholism could be ended with that one word.

I was reminded of the spiritual power of the Serenity Prayer again this morning when my mind was boggled by a family situation I want fixed now. I said only the first word, "God," and once again that wave of relief swept over me. I don't have to do this alone.

—*Connecticut, United States*

Dear God, I am powerless and my life is unmanageable without Your help and guidance. I come to You today because I believe that You can restore and renew me to meet my needs today. Since I cannot manage my life or affairs, I have decided to give them to You. I put my life, my will, my thoughts, my desires and ambitions in Your hands.

I give You all of me: the good and the bad, the character defects and shortcomings, my selfishness, resentments and problems. I know that You will work them out in accordance with Your plan. Such as I am, take and use me in Your service. Guide and direct my ways and show me what to do for You.

I cannot control or change my friends or loved ones, so I release them into Your care for Your loving hands to do with as You will. Just keep me loving and free from judging them. If they need changing, God, You'll have to do it; I can't. Just make me willing and ready to be of service to You, to have my shortcomings removed, and to do my best.

Help me to see how I have harmed others and make me willing to make amends to them all. Keep me ever mindful of thoughts and actions that harm myself and others, and which separate me from Your light, love and spirit. And when I commit these errors, make me aware of them and help me to admit each one promptly.

I am seeking to know You better, to love You more. I am seeking the knowledge of Your will for me and the power to carry it out.

—*Anonymous*

Lord, teach me patience, and remind me that it

is hard work, but well worth my labor. Guide me in all I do to remember that waiting is the answer to some of my prayers, and that when I need You, You will be there to help me.

—*Florida, United States*

Dear God, forgive me for doubting that You are working to bring about the very best in my life. I know that I have been fearful, for I have sought to take care of my own problems instead of asking for Your help. When I doubt, would you please get my mind off my fears and help me to remember that You are the power that can bring about miracles in my life.

I've taken so many things for granted, so now I am asking You for a grateful heart that yields in service to others who are in pain. Free me from the desire to change others and help me to love myself, even as You so perfectly love me.

Help me to learn from the past so that I will not continue to make the same mistakes over and over again. Let me be aware of Your presence daily. Help me keep my inventory up-to-date, making proper amends, minute by minute, as I need to.

Thank you for showing me love in action in Al-Anon groups. Thank You for meeting all of my needs and for showing me that I need You and Your power each day of my life.

Thank You for the miracle that You are performing in my life and for giving me the gift of life itself.

—*West Virginia and Utah, United States*

Meditation is not what you think.
—*Indiana, United States*

I have been able through meditation to get a feeling of closeness with the tide of life that surrounds me and sustains me. I can hear heartbeats instead of drum beats, and I am aware of an ever-deepening rhythm of life. I have had an occasional consciousness of the eternal life force that makes grass grow and all living things kin. I can become part of this wholeness that is greater than myself but to which I belong. I can look up at the sky each morning and see its continuing miracle.

—*New York, United States*

I learned a form of meditation during spiritual questioning long before I learned about Al-Anon, and the practice is even more helpful since it has become a part of my program. I meditate whenever and wherever I can quite often. I even find myself meditating in the bathtub. It is quiet and I can expect at least a few moments of uninterrupted solitude. I try to relax my body completely and "empty" my mind. I close my eyes and try to shut out thoughts, words, external sensations and consciousness of time. This takes practice and I am not always able to do it, but when I achieve that feeling of being one with all that is around me, I feel good and whole and at peace. Sometimes, I am able to do this while

I am washing the dishes or listening to the news. It may only take five minutes, but I find that it makes me look at the world differently when I do it. When I "come back to the world," I am refreshed, drained of all negative emotions and filled with calm acceptance.

—*Wisconsin, United States*

My husband's alcoholism progressed and so did my anger at God. I had never been "bad," so why was I being punished? Why did my husband still drink? No answers came, and I stopped believing in God.

One day, I received an answer, although I didn't recognize it at the time. I had a moment of sanity when I saw my situation and the degeneration of my life clearly. All I could say was, "God help me."

For the first time, I didn't tell God how to help, and I knew I needed help. Help came because I found and became involved in Al-Anon. I began to see that my behavior was a problem, so I took the focus off my husband and put it on myself. My life improved and many problems were resolved when I used the tools of the program.

Years later, I came face-to-face with prayer and meditation in the Eleventh Step. I was forced to look at this aspect of my life in an entirely new way. For me, the Eleventh Step can never have a place without the first three Steps. Through accepting powerlessness and unmanageability over alcohol, realizing a Higher Power could restore sanity and manageability, and turning my life and my will over to that power, I had found the "something" I had always lacked. I found a Higher Power to be a moving force in my daily life.

This was proven over and over as I turned my situations over to the Higher Power. I had begun to pray again without realizing it. I would talk the situation over with the Higher Power before turning it over and letting go. I began asking not for my answer—or the comfortable answer, the secure answer, the easy answer—but for the best answer, whatever the consequences.

In between times of turning things over, my mind was still whirling. At an Eleventh Step meeting, I found an answer: meditation. At first, my reaction was negative due to my past experiences with meditation. I had found it to be tedious, boring, repetitious and unsatisfying. But my sponsor encouraged me to try to take a quiet time just to stop whirling.

My regular meditation today is a necessity. I have to take time to listen and learn what's good for me today. I read a spiritual passage and try to apply it to my life; I ask guidance of the Higher Power and then spend time just thinking and listening. Ideas come to me that I know are from a Power greater than myself, and I often write these thoughts in a special notebook. It's sometimes difficult to concentrate on spiritual ideas. I know I have to separate the time necessary for planning my day from the time necessary to center my life. When I care enough for myself to set aside this time, I have given myself a gift. I've given myself a chance to center my life, not as it was for so long in confusion, but in the care of a loving Higher Power who helps direct and guide my life through the spiritual principles of Al-Anon.

—*New York, United States*

`I remember how excited and joyous I was inwardly when I discovered the Eleventh Step. I was very undisciplined in my prayer and knew nothing of meditation, but I was willing and eager to learn how to do it, and I did.

For a long time, I had a continuing nightmare that haunted me. I had had the same dream since childhood, and I never knew when it would come and terrify me again. As I started to meditate, my dreams gradually changed. I remember hearing, in meditation, that when the scary monster reared its ugly head again, I should close my eyes and pray. I knew that this would be difficult in my dream state, but I was determined to try it, and I continually prayed to the Higher Power for His support and the strength to do this.

One night, the monster appeared to me in my dream and I remembered clearly what I had heard in meditation, so I prayed. Then, to my great surprise, the "monster" turned to gold dust and became a part of me as I was praying. I awakened feeling refreshed and thankful to the Higher Power.

—*California, United States*

We can find peace of mind and real fulfillment only through devotion to something above and beyond ourselves.

—*North Carolina, United States*

Meditation must be, I think, a conscious act and not a sort of dreaming. Meditation can bring quietness and serenity in a period of emotional troubles if we succeed in concentrating on the chosen subject. This, of course, is not so easy, and it needs to be practiced regularly, One Day at a Time.

—*France*

Long before a baby knows that it has a stomach, it wants to eat. Similarly, I believe that our spiritual hungers seek satisfaction, even if we don't always know what or how to feed them. The hunger cries within us until it is satisfied with proper nourishment. We may look for satisfaction in excess food, materialistic obsessions, compulsive housecleaning, or attempts to control other external events in our lives.

But the hunger is internal; the soul seeks to be united with the Creator. My spiritual hunger is only satisfied by making contact with my Higher Power each day, seeking to know Its true nature and asking for knowledge of Its will for me and the power to carry it out.

—*Michigan, United States*

On a transcontinental flight, cruising at 39,000 feet, the phrase, "Nearer my God to Thee" came to mind. I felt peaceful and close to my Higher Power and wondered why.

The sun was millions of miles away, and I wasn't about to meet some angels out on an excursion from heaven. It wasn't where I was, but how I was.

First, I was content to be where I was in the time and space. One of the joys of traveling is that feeling of here and now. Whatever I didn't do or pack before I left, it was too late to worry about it and too early to start anything awaiting me at my destination. Time and space were suspended. The hours on my wristwatch were meaningless. My only points of reference were the captain's voice on the loud speaker and the view from the window.

Looking out, I saw the vast stretches of the Plains' states, the snow-covered checkerboard fields and winding rivers. The formidable mountains became merely fascinating patterns of gray and white, hardly more forbidding than the gray mounds of snow in the city after a heavy snowstorm.

My view of my personal world was also totally different. The continuing concerns were reduced to small squares, easily crossed with one jump. The big problems flattened out, like the mountains, to dark smudges. There was serenity in that objectivity.

Probably the most significant factor in my serenity was the realization that whatever happened on the flight, I was totally powerless to affect the outcome. All I had to do was keep my seat belt fastened.

Living in the present moment, taking an objective view of my life and accepting my total powerlessness, even over possible disaster, were the things that had brought me nearer to the God of my understanding. If I can follow those precepts when my legs are firmly planted on the ground, I will be able to live the Eleventh Step, increasing my conscious contact with God.

—New York, United States

I think I've developed an understanding of God that I don't fully understand.

—*Texas, United States*

Through daily prayer and meditation, my relationship with God, to whom I have given the care of my life and my will, is a happy, comfortable one. Each day when I ask for knowledge of His will for me and the power to carry that out, I am reminded of the decision I made in the Third Step. I have come to know that what happens in a day's time is His will for me and somehow, in some way, best for me. My spiritual growth has been slow but I hope, continuing. I shall never reach perfection. I do not strive for it, only for a little progress each day as I try to carry the message to others and to practice the principles of all of the Steps in all of my affairs. So long as I do this, I am on the road to recovery. It's a never-ending road, but not a tiresome one, because around every curve is a new happiness.

—*Louisiana, United States*

May the storms of life be gentle showers and the light of God's love shine brightly upon your pathway.

—*South Carolina, United States*

7

Practicing The Spiritual Life

Step Twelve states: "Having had a spiritual awakening as the result of these Steps, we tried to carry this message to others and to practice these principles in all our affairs." When we were new in the program this seemed an impossible task, but as we progressed in working and understanding the Steps, the meaning of the Twelfth Step became more apparent. A member from South Carolina writes: "I have grown enough in the program that I try not to see difficult days as filled with problems, but days to live and grow. When I do, it's a lot easier for me to realize that *this is life* and I'm doing a lot of living." Working the Twelve Steps brings us to a fuller understanding of the ways that we can use the program "in all our affairs." While it is true that what brings us to Al-Anon is the pain of dealing with another person's alcoholism, what keeps us coming back is the serenity we gain when we learn how to make our lives manageable.

For many of us, the true value of the program becomes obvious as we discover that we are able to practice these principles not only with our family members, but with our employers and co-workers, neighbors, and even casual acquaintances. We are able to make plans, work toward goals, and live our lives purposefully. Before Al-Anon, many of us were so caught up in our fears and negative emotions that we wasted several years that we can never regain. Now we are able to live without regrets, in a way that becomes rewarding and self-reinforcing. We are able to do what we have to do to act in a responsible way. Once we begin living in the Tenth, Eleventh and Twelfth Steps on a daily basis, we are able to live lives of "sane and happy usefulness." We have no desire to return to the past with its pain, anger and frustration. We learn to make choices which will lead us to satisfaction and fulfillment. This chapter focuses on the far-reaching changes in attitudes and behavior which have resulted from this program and the spiritual awakenings of its members.

The Twelve Steps have allowed us to see life with a new vision, to realize that we are able to live happily and sanely today, and that God's will for us is to make a contribution to the peace of other people who are traveling this path with us. We who have lived in anguish for so long have discovered a way to live in serenity, One Day at a Time, and our greatest joy is to share this way of life with others.

The first definition of "spirit" in *Webster's Unabridged Dictionary* is "the breath of life . . . a breath or vapor which animates the soul of man." That's what spirituality is all about for me—being alive with a spirit that animates all that I do. For me, spiritual growth has resulted in a tremendous feeling of freedom—freedom to be, to do, to feel, to express those feelings. I feel alive now. How different from my "former life" when I felt so closed off from life through fear and lack of self-esteem. Being alive means that I have choices and I make choices.

True, I have been making choices all along. Denying the alcoholism was a choice. Hiding from risk was a choice. Closing myself off from love was a choice. And attending Al-Anon was a choice—one which opened the door to the crucial choice of the Twelve Steps as my personal path to growth of the spirit.

As I have worked through the Steps and applied the principles of the program on a daily basis, this spirit has gently taken hold of my life, shaping my decisions and presenting me with opportunities for continuing growth. As panic and confusion subside, and as I learn to trust this spirit and trust myself to act in my best interests, I make better and better choices: choices that lead me to fuller enjoyment of all that life has to offer me; choices that allow the long-hidden, bubbly side of my personality to emerge.

"Bubbly" is the perfect word to describe what I feel now. A few years ago, I visited Yellowstone National Park, the location of Old Faithful. The park also has numerous "Little Faithfuls," which bubble up all over the place when "the spirit moves them." People wait in crowds to witness the phenomenon, based on a schedule of approximate eruption times which are posted daily. But these geysers just bubble when they are ready, when the mysterious geological forces which cause the eruptions combine in such a way that the pressure must find release.

That's how it is for me these days—the spirit bubbles when it will. As I trust this spirit and let it out, good things happen. I certainly feel more relaxed and more fulfilled. All the stress of repression is lifted, and the energy which I once used to repress myself is now free to be applied to living more fully in the present, to focus on future goals, to anticipate, to make plans, to make commitments, to make choices. How often in the past I let confusion and emotional turmoil influence me to avoid choices. Now, I use my future goals to shape the decisions I make today.

But the true freedom is spontaneity—the freedom to be flexible, to seize the moment of opportunity and run with it. With trust in a Higher Power, surrender to His care and prayer for knowledge of His will for me and the power to carry that out, I believe that I can continue to grow spiritually One Day at a Time, not without pain and challenge, but certainly with serenity. Truly, my life "bubbles" over.

—*New York, United States*

To me, Al-Anon had many, many answers to deal with the practical problems of living with a practicing alcoholic husband in the later stages of the disease, just as it has many answers now that I am widowed as the result of alcoholism taking its toll on my husband's sanity and life.

Al-Anon has given me a spiritual awakening. It has resulted in a growth surprising and confusing in its scope. Its power to restore me to healthy well-being and serene contentment is far beyond what I could ever have imagined, regardless of how difficult the atmosphere around me, in days when very few, if any, lives are free from the problems of living.

I find that my appreciation and understanding of my own faith has grown to a remarkable extent. Though I no longer feel an outcast, I do feel different, and value it, because the difference I feel is growth. In both Al-Anon and my church, I have become aware of the regard in which I am held by the God of my new understanding. Traditional values, which I once held only by unthinking habit of mind, are now part of my life. In the past, the goodness of life was dimly perceived, but now I see its goodness clearly and life itself has been restored to me with great vitality and beauty.

—*Australia*

To me, the beauty of the Al-Anon program is that it applies to life in general. It helps me stand firm in any emergency; it gives me a new appreciation of life and it helps me realize that it is not important what happens in my life, it's how I deal with the events and how I meet whatever comes my way. I stopped my childish fantasies and Al-Anon directed me to an orderly, meaningful life and showed me how to attain this and keep it at last. I began to mature instead of being overwhelmed by fears and ghosts of the past. Today, I ask for guidance and pray that I will be a better person today than I was yesterday and that I will meet each day's challenges in a sane manner. When I reflect on the day's events, and know that I have functioned the best I can, I am at peace. The pieces of the puzzle of my life all center around why I found Al-Anon. It has helped me live sanely despite the alcoholism in others close to me.

—*New York, United States*

In a daily review of my attitudes and actions, I look for the qualities I want to change in myself—the times during the day when either my attitude or my behavior was inappropriate. I ask myself whether I am in harmony with what I believe is God's will for me. How is my serenity? Is my thinking reasonably sane? Are my relationships with my family smooth and flowing? How about my relationships with others? Where am I failing to "practice these principles in all my affairs?" Do I spend time and energy "tilting at windmills" instead of practicing acceptance? Then I ask myself how I can do things differently tomorrow. I either make or resolve to make amends that are necessary.

I also look for guidance of any good qualities during my review. I look for the things that I've done well and for attitudes that are changing or have changed. I look for progress. There was a time when nothing less then perfection counted. Today, progress counts! These are the qualities I want to reinforce in me because they are my building blocks and I can use these good qualities to continue building on the good foundation I am establishing.

Step Ten gives me a choice. I can use it to focus on my defects of character day after day, never changing, or I can use it for change and growth by giving my defects to God and keeping my focus on Him and the good that is growing in me.

—*Texas, United States*

I was in Al-Anon for about four years when I received a call at work and was informed that my 15-year-old child was in jail. As I was walking to my car, I put this trouble in the First Step and I worked on the belief that a "Higher Power" could help, and I turned that trouble over to the "Higher Power."

As I drove the 50 miles from work to the jail, I said the Serenity Prayer, "Easy Does It," "Let Go and Let God," and "One Day at a Time." I said them over and over; these were the only thoughts that I would allow myself to think.

The first thing I noticed when joining other family members at the jail was that my emotional and mental condition was different than theirs. I was calm and rational, and let me tell you, they were not. This difference was noticeable to my child, who turned to me for support as soon as I arrived.

I felt wonderment and relief. The trouble was minor; we were bridging the gap caused by the family illness of alcoholism, and I had found a Higher Power. I no longer had to "act as if" I believed.

I had started working the Second and Third Steps, not out of faith or belief, but because it worked for other people and maybe "It" would work for me. And I believe "It" did.

—*Anonymous*

I am learning to overcome my natural tendency to react to what other people say or do. For when I react, I put control of my peace of mind in their hands. I am glad to know that serenity is under my control and I don't have to relinquish it for trivial occurrences.

—*Montana, United States*

My gift from the Al-Anon program is that it has guided me to a recovery that is beyond "acceptable insanity." I work in a large city and there are several eccentric characters who wander the streets downtown. One of them walks around constantly muttering to himself. Sometimes he talks calmly and makes sense and sometimes he becomes agitated and spouts obscenities. The only difference between him and me is that he externalizes his thoughts so others can hear them.

Similarly, there is another character who walks around town, pushing a shopping cart filled with his belongings, many of which have been scavenged from trash bins. I see him and realize that the only difference between us is that he carries his garbage out where everyone can see it.

These two people gave me great insight into myself and helped me to realize that most folks are living in "acceptable insanity." Our condition was acceptable until it got too painful or we got too violent.

Today, I know that my mind wanders from making sense to obsessing. And I know that there is still mind garbage to get rid of, though far, far less then there used to be. Al-Anon has given me a program to deal with my obsessions, to sort out the garbage, and get on with a meaningful life. Furthermore, it has allowed me a quality of life which I never would have thought possible. It has enabled me to achieve a level of mental health that goes beyond "acceptable insanity." This quality of life and mental health are contingent upon my maintaining a fit spiritual condition and sharing my program with others.

—*Indiana, United States*

When I see a newcomer at a meeting, crying and blaming herself for the actions and reactions of all those around her and trying her best to satisfy all their demands, I remember what I was like when I came into this fellowship. I see her pain and I am grateful that, for today, I no longer have to judge my behavior and feelings by the opinions of others and I do not have to feel responsible for the actions of others, no matter how close we are to each other.

Today, I can make healthy, life-giving, life-affirming, choices for myself. If I find myself reacting to emotional frenzy in others, I can remove myself from the situation or I can contribute calmness and assurance that even the worst problems have a way of coming to a resolution. I know that no problem lasts forever, so I no longer feel that urgent need to find the perfect solution in the next ten minutes.

I have learned to share my problems with others. I no longer have to make decisions without benefit of the insight and experience of others who have traveled a similar path. Through Al-Anon, I have met many people who are living lives of "sane and happy usefulness." Before Al-Anon, almost everyone I knew was in deep emotional pain and had no resources for me to draw upon. I learned that I could not make healthy choices by basing decisions on unhealthy role models. Even if I chose a course of action opposite to theirs, so as to avoid their mistakes, there was no guarantee that I was making the right decision. Even with the counsel of Al-Anon members, I may make unwise decisions; but with their guidance, I can admit that I am human, I make mistakes, and I can go on from where I am. I do not have to stay in indecision and misery.

This exposure to sane and happy people has

made my relationships with the "crazies" in my life much easier. When I see people close to me make what I believe are foolish decisions, I can say "Live and Let Live." In the unlikely event that they ask for my opinion, I can offer it, but what they do with it is their decision. I cannot take it as an affront if they choose a different course of action than I would. After all, they do not have the benefits of this program.

Today, I can turn them over to God. When I was in that newcomer's shoes, I felt terribly responsible for the actions of those who were close to me. The alcoholic in my life continually threatened to "blow up" himself and City Hall and as many people as he could take with him. I could not imagine how I could live with myself if he did that. Thankfully, I never had to find out. But in Al-Anon, I learned that even if he had done that, nothing I could have done or said could have prevented it. It is not in our power to control the actions, attitudes or disease of another human being. Only God can heal him and direct his path.

The Twelve Steps of our program have led me to a faith in God today which is based on acceptance of the world as it is. I no longer agonize over how the world should be. God created this world and I am responsible for using my talents and gifts to make a positive contribution to the world today. After all if the world were a perfect place, how could I, an imperfect being, feel like I was making an important contribution to it? God, as I understand Him, has led me through this life and given me the gifts of acceptance and faith and it is up to me to share them with others.

—*Ohio, United States*

Emerging out of a cocoon of being dependent on others was hard work. Breaking all the threads that sheltered and protected me through the years was scary. When I cut one of those protective threads, I just knew that I would fall and land in a place that was not very safe. Learning who I was and what I needed and wanted was a slow process of learning and re-learning. I was terrified I would lose the relationships that meant the most to me. My mistakes seemed monstrous and huge, overshadowing the small amount of progress I was acquiring for myself.

Slowly, as I began to emerge from this cocoon, I felt like a film was being removed and my sight was being restored. Through this program, I was led to the help I needed for myself. I began to see more things I liked about myself than I disliked. I was amazed to discover how I had depended on others for my security, my well-being and my happiness. I let others make my decisions for me. I knew all the ways to get someone to do just that. If my cocoon was threatened, I drew up tight inside of it and withdrew from others for awhile.

I am the one who built the webs around myself. This program has enabled me to get rid of that cocoon. With God's help and guidance, I am growing wings. My relationships are more meaningful. My world is broader. My faith is deeper; I respect myself more. I do not have to live in your image anymore; therefore, I can see who you are, too. Sight restored, my hearing got better too. I can hear what you like, what you need, without being threatened. I can learn from you and retain my uniqueness. I can share with you and not expect you to live in my image.

Today, I am building on the good qualities I have. Taking a look at the things that obstruct my own growth and accepting the whole of me, knowing the things I still do not like about myself, I can change, with faith and patience. I know this is true because I have the experience of the changes I have already made behind me. This program really works and it never ceases to amaze me.

—*Scotland*

The shell that had enclosed my life, that had prevented me from living and loving, has cracked, and the power of the Al-Anon program is filling the void that for years kept me at a distance from life. I was an observer, but now I am a participant.

—*New York, United States*

After a number of years in the program, my wife and I were starting to face our marriage more honestly. The most honest communication came one bright spring afternoon when my wife said it was time we talked. I knew this was serious because she called me by my given name and that was always a sign of seriousness.

We decided to take a walk and talk things out. I immediately started repeating the Serenity Prayer and "Let Go and Let God" to myself. I also turned the results, whatever they might be, over to my Higher Power, and asked for acceptance.

The result of our walking and talking was a decision to end our marriage. My wife told me that she didn't love me and had never loved me. Of course, this is not what I wanted to hear; I wanted to hear that we were in love and would live happily ever after. For years, I had longed for an honest, straightforward relationship, and now we had just that. I felt a great calm come over me and a new kind of love for my wife. This love had no romance or possessiveness in it. This was love from my Higher Power.

I also felt a great loss because, after 20 years of marriage and the growth we had attained through our programs, our time together was finished.

It has been three and a half years since our walk and I still feel the calmness and love of my Higher Power. I believe that She has boundless love which I will always feel as long as I stay in fit spiritual conditions, and She will help me maintain my spiritual awakening.

As a result of making the decision to say in this program for life, I had a wonderful woman enter my life. After dating and sharing many meetings together, it became obvious to us that we could share a loving, honest, straightforward marriage together. All the subtleties of a healthy relationship which we both knew we were capable of, were coming true for us. So we were married. And we know that our Higher Power is sharing Her love with us.

—*Indiana, United States*

The lives of all human beings are composed of different phases and each phase represents a new beginning. Each phase is like a season of the year, different, yet transient. If we live these seasons consciously, we can enjoy the winter as well as the spring.

When Al-Anon came into my life, I learned that there are always opportunities for a new beginning. The good and bad experiences of the past helped me to recognize my mistakes, to start making appropriate changes and enjoy the results. I was able to give and receive love, respect, understanding, peace and serenity in a home where there had only been tears, screams, insults and threats. The years went by and the children grew up and started to get married—

another new beginning. I learned to respect them as adults and to enjoy my grandchildren. Then, after 32 years of marriage, my husband left and remarried. Now, I have another new beginning. I have learned to accept reality and to adapt myself to it, to get rid of resentments, to live alone, and to enjoy everything I have, which I think is enough, because I have my life. I am fulfilled. I am the owner of my time, my space, and myself. I enjoy the visits of my children and my grandchildren. I have discovered that after a cloudy day, the sun shines in all its magnificence so I can see everything God has created for me. I have a big family in Al-Anon. I may live alone, but I am no longer lonely. A new season is fast approaching, but I have a program to help me deal with old age and it will help me look at every day as a new beginning.

—*Mexico*

I was listening to a man discuss the problems in his family which resulted from unemployment. One of the problems which he seemed to consider most serious was that the family had to give up their snowmobile and a few other luxury items. I caught myself being judgmental and sneering at his concept of deprivation. I thought of all the people who could live their whole lives without a snowmobile and never miss it. I have traveled in parts of the world where the majority of its people would be grateful for a meal or a place of shelter or even a drink of fresh water. And this man was feeling sorry for himself about giving up a snowmobile!

Then I realized that I was reacting to his self-pity. As a result of the Al-Anon program, I have learned that self-pity is crippling. For me, it clouded reality. It prevented me from seeing anything positive in my life. And suddenly, I felt compassion, not because he was deprived of a snowmobile, but because he was dwelling in the negativity I was released from after working the Al-Anon program.

—*Michigan, United States*

Early last autumn, when I visited my daughter in Vermont, we climbed Mount Humger, 2,250 feet high. We started off through lovely, thick woods of tall oaks and white birches where we could see nothing except the trail ahead of us. As it wound up the mountain and we came to look-outs, we gradually could scan the upper branch-es of trees we had already passed. When it seemed as though we should surely be at the top, we suddenly encountered steep rock walls. Getting over them gave us a new view. Finally, at the summit, we could look out over the valley and a new world was spread before us with the horizon pushed even farther back.

Our perception had suddenly changed. Instead of being attracted to rich green mosses on the forest floor and sunlight filtering onto tree trunks, we saw the wide sweep of the receding mountain ranges, Lake Champlain shimmering off to the west, and light clouds moving in front of the sun.

Our progress in Al-Anon gives us this same

opportunity to broaden our vistas of ourselves and our world. When I first came to Al-Anon, I felt as though I was in a thicket that could only be hacked through with a machete. Walking up the Steps of the program, I began to get some space. I could see where I was. Instead of focusing on the immediate crises, I could take a longer look.

Even more, I could begin to see myself differently and let go of limiting beliefs about myself. Each time I applied a slogan or understood a Step at a different level, I was no longer caught in fear and self-doubt, but could move ahead more boldly. I had a higher vantage point. This is the spiritual awakening available through the Twelve Steps.

A Tibetan writer, Djwhal Kahul, has said that everything is spiritual which tends toward understanding, toward kindness, toward that which is productive of beauty and leads man on to a fuller expression of his divine potential. Each advance we make in personal insight and awareness of others is spiritual growth. We can leave the thickets of distrust and discouragement and climb up where we have new worlds at our feet and far horizons before us.

—*New York, United States*

I watched her walk up the short, curved walk from her car in my driveway to my front door. There was no bounce in her step and her shoulders drooped. Silently, I said, "Please give me a listening heart and the right words to say." As I answered the door, she smiled, but the smile seemed stitched in place. We had a cup of coffee and talked; her words were rehearsed and she was minimizing the problems. I knew because I had once been like her. Finally, I said, "I understand, and I care." Then she began to talk more freely and the words tumbled out. I told her about Al-Anon and what it had done for me and what I believed it could do for her. I told her that she was powerless over alcohol and over any person except herself.

When I walked with her to the door, she did not say, "I'll be at the meeting Monday night," as I had hoped she would, but she did say, "I'll be in touch." I noticed that her smile seemed more genuine, there was no longer a pronounced droop in her shoulders, and she had a bit of a spring in her step. Silently, I said, "Thank You. I believe we helped."

For her and so many others like her, I am responsible. Let It Begin With Me.

—*Louisiana, United States*

Acknowledgments

While it was not possible to acknowledge all sources, we are grateful to the Al-Anon writer/editor and to other editors of area newsletters and magazines from around the world, and to all members for their contributions to this book.

The Twelve Steps

1. We admitted we were powerless over alcohol—that our lives had become unmanageable.
2. Came to believe that a Power greater than ourselves could restore us to sanity.
3. Made a decision to turn our will and our lives over to the care of God *as we understood Him.*
4. Made a searching and fearless moral inventory of ourselves.
5. Admitted to God, to ourselves, and to another human being the exact nature of our wrongs.
6. Were entirely ready to have God remove all these defects of character.

7. Humbly asked Him to remove our short-comings.

8. Made a list of all persons we had harmed, and became willing to make amends to them all.

9. Made direct amends to such people wherever possible, except when to do so would injure them or others.

10. Continued to take personal inventory and when we were wrong promptly admitted it.

11. Sought through prayer and meditation to improve our conscious contact with God *as we understood Him*, praying only for knowledge of His will for us and the power to carry that out.

12. Having had a spiritual awakening as the result of these Steps, we tried to carry this message to others, and to practice these principles in all our affairs.

The Twelve Traditions

1. Our common welfare should come first; personal progress for the greatest number depends upon unity.

2. For our group purpose there is but one authority—a loving God as He may express Himself in our group conscience. Our leaders are but trusted servants; they do not govern.

3. The relatives of alcoholics, when gathered together for mutual aid, may call themselves an Al-Anon Family Group, provided that, as a group, they have no other affiliation. The only requirement for membership is that there be a problem of alcoholism in a relative or friend.

4. Each group should be autonomous, except in matters affecting another group or Al-Anon or AA as a whole.

5. Each Al-Anon Family Group has but one purpose: to help families of alcoholics. We do this by practicing the Twelve Steps of AA *ourselves*, by encouraging and understanding our alcoholic relatives, and by welcoming and giving comfort to families of alcoholics.

6. Our Al-Anon Family Groups ought never endorse, finance or lend our name to any outside enterprise, lest problems of money, property and prestige divert us from our primary spiritual aim. Although a separate entity, we should always cooperate with Alcoholics Anonymous.

7. Every group ought to be fully self-supporting, declining outside contributions.

8. Al-Anon Twelfth-Step work should remain forever non-professional, but our service centers may employ special workers.

9. Our groups, as such, ought never be organized; but we may create service boards or committees directly responsible to those they serve.

10. The Al-Anon Family Groups have no opinion on outside issues; hence our name ought never be drawn into public controversy.

11. Our public relations policy is based on attraction rather than promotion; we need always maintain personal anonymity at the level of press, radio, TV and films. We need guard with special care the anonymity of all AA members.

12. Anonymity is the spiritual foundation of all our Traditions, ever reminding us to place principles above personalities.

Al-Anon's Twelve
Concepts of Service

The Twelve Steps and Traditions are guides for personal growth and group unity. The Twelve Concepts are guides for service. They show how Twelfth Step work can be done on a broad scale and how members of a World Service Office can relate to each other and to the groups, through a World Service Conference, to spread Al-Anon's message worldwide.

1. The ultimate responsibility and authority for Al-Anon world services belongs to the Al-Anon groups.
2. The Al-Anon Family Groups have delegated complete administrative and operational authority to their Conference and its service arms.
3. The Right of Decision makes effective leadership possible.
4. Participation is the key to harmony.

5. The Rights of Appeal and Petition protect minorities and assure that they be heard.

6. The Conference acknowledges the primary administrative responsibility of the trustees.

7. The trustees have legal rights while the rights of the Conference are traditional.

8. The Board of Trustees delegates full authority for routine management of the Al-Anon Headquarters to its executive committees.

9. Good personal leadership at all service levels is a necessity. In the field of world service the Board of Trustees assumes the primary leadership.

10. Service responsibility is balanced by carefully defined service authority and double-headed management is avoided.

11. The World Service Office is composed of standing committees, executives and staff members.

12. The spiritual foundation for Al-Anon's world service is contained in the General Warranties of the Conference, Article 12 of the Charter.

General Warranties

In all its proceedings the World Service Conference of Al-Anon shall observe the spirit of the Traditions:

1. *that only sufficient operating funds, including an ample reserve, be its prudent financial principle;*

2. *that no Conference member shall be placed in unqualified authority over other members;*

3. *that all decisions be reached by discussion, vote and, whenever possible, by unanimity;*

4. *that no Conference action ever be personally punitive or an incitement to public controversy;*

5. *that though the Conference serves Al-Anon, it shall never perform any act of government; and that, like the fellowship of Al-Anon Family Groups which it serves, it shall always remain democratic in thought and action.*

INDEX

267